To Live
Forever

To Live Forever

Egyptian Treasures from the Brooklyn Museum

Edward Bleiberg

With an essay by
Kathlyn M. Cooney

Brooklyn Museum in association with D Giles Limited, London

Published on the occasion of the traveling exhibition *To Live Forever: Egyptian Treasures from the Brooklyn Museum*, organized by the Brooklyn Museum from its collections

First published in 2008 by GILES
an imprint of D Giles Limited
2nd Floor
162–164 Upper Richmond Road, London, SW15 2SL, UK
www.gilesltd.com

Library of Congress Cataloging-in-Publication Data

Brooklyn Museum.
   To Live forever : Egyptian treasures from the Brooklyn Museum / Edward Bleiberg ; with an essay by Kathlyn M. Cooney.
      p. cm.
   Includes bibliographical references and index.
   ISBN 978-0-87273-159-2 (pbk. : alk. paper) – ISBN 978-1-904832-52-2 (hardcover : alk. paper)
   1. Egypt–Antiquities–Catalogs. 2. Art, Egyptian–Catalogs. 3. Funeral rites and ceremonies–Egypt–Catalogs. I. Bleiberg, Edward, 1951- II. Cooney, Kathlyn M. III. Title.
   DT59.N733B76 2008
   932.0074'74723--dc22   2007031035

ISBN paperback: 978-0-87273-159-2
ISBN hardback: 978-1-904832-52-2

For the Brooklyn Museum
Edited by James Leggio, Head of Publications and Editorial Services
Principal digital photography by Sarah Kraemer and Christine Gant

For D Giles Limited
Proofread by John Gilbert and David Rose
Designed by Mercer Design, London
Produced by GILES, an imprint of D Giles Limited, London
Printed and bound in China

Exhibition Itinerary

Indianapolis Museum of Art, Indianapolis, Indiana

John and Mable Ringling Museum of Art, Sarasota, Florida

Columbus Museum of Art, Columbus, Ohio

Chrysler Museum of Art, Norfolk, Virginia

Norton Museum of Art, West Palm Beach, Florida

Frist Center for the Visual Arts, Nashville, Tennessee

Front cover: Detail of *Mummy Mask of a Man* (see fig. 106)

Back cover: Detail of *Coffin of the Lady of the House, Weretwahset, Reinscribed for Bensuipet* (see fig. 124)

Frontispiece: *Shabty of Amunemhat* (see fig. 7)

Page 7: Ruins of the temple at Deir el-Medina, Egypt

Pages 8, 108–109, 142–143: Sites in the Valley of the Kings, west bank of the Nile at Luxor (ancient Thebes), Egypt

Page 22: *Block Statue of a High Official*. From Karnak, Egypt. Ptolemaic Period, 305–30 B.C.E. Diorite, 15 ⅜ x 6 ⁹⁄₁₆ x 7 ⅞ in. (39 x 16.7 x 20 cm). Charles Edwin Wilbour Fund, 69.115.1

Page 110: *Jar Lid with Human Face* (see fig. 79)

Contents

Foreword

Life after death was a primary cultural belief through thousands of years of Egyptian history. The ancient Egyptians regarded death as an enemy that could be defeated through the insurance of proper preparation. *To Live Forever* draws on the superb collection of the Brooklyn Museum to illustrate Egyptian strategies for defeating death and living forever.

This book and exhibition answer the questions at the core of the public's fascination with ancient Egypt, as they explain the Egyptians' beliefs about death and the afterlife, the process of mummification, the conduct of a funeral, and the different types of tombs. At the same time, *To Live Forever* offers an innovative approach to these beliefs by addressing the practical, economic considerations an ancient Egyptian faced when preparing for the next world—an ancient form of insurance for the afterlife. And it deals with the afterlife preparations not only of kings and nobles, but also of the middle class and the poor. It thus offers a fresh take on a perennially fascinating subject. It is our hope that *To Live Forever* will lead new audiences to value and understand Egyptian art, engaging visitors across a wide spectrum of interests while advancing the Museum's tradition of scholarship.

I am grateful to Edward Bleiberg, Curator of Egyptian, Classical, and Ancient Middle Eastern Art, for conceiving of this project and bringing it so handsomely to realization. His curatorial intelligence has guided the project throughout its development.

As always, in addition to the organizing curator, many members of the Brooklyn Museum's staff have collaborated to produce this magnificent exhibition and catalogue. Special thanks go to Radiah Harper, James Leggio, Kenneth Moser, Matthew Yokobosky, and the teams they lead. Conservators Lisa Bruno, Rachel Danzing, Jakki Godfrey, Tina March, and Toni Owen worked tirelessly to prepare these ancient artifacts for exhibition. The majority of the photographs reproduced in this volume were taken specially for this project by staff photographers Sarah Kraemer and Christine Gant. Kathy Zurek rendered invaluable services to the exhibition.

For the ongoing support of the Museum's Trustees, we extend special gratitude to Norman Feinberg, Chairman, and every member of our Board. Without the confidence and active engagement of our Trustees, it would not be possible to initiate and maintain the high level of exhibition and publication programming exemplified by *To Live Forever*.

Arnold L. Lehman
Director, Brooklyn Museum

A Brief Chronology of Ancient Egypt

This chronology is intended to help readers navigate the vast tract of time known as ancient Egyptian history. The chronology outlines the development of Egyptian civilization through its many periods and comments briefly on the historical features of each principal era.

Egyptologists divide Egyptian history into eleven major periods. Over the centuries, periods of strong central government, or kingdoms, alternate with intermediate eras of weaker central authority and reliance on local rule. In the Prehistoric Period (5000–4400 B.C.E.), most people were farmers and there was no central government. The Predynastic Period (4400–3000 B.C.E.) reveals traits that anticipate classical Egyptian culture and customs. The Early Dynastic Period (3000–2675 B.C.E.) witnessed the first centralized government in Egypt. The next period, the Old Kingdom (2675–2170 B.C.E.), is often called the Pyramid Age and produced the best-known monuments of ancient Egypt. Centralized government dissolved at the end of the Old Kingdom, leading to the First Intermediate Period (2170–2008 B.C.E.), a transitional era that existed "between kingdoms" and was marked by local rule. After it followed the Middle Kingdom (2008–1630 B.C.E.), a time of renewed central government and impressive artistic and literary production. A second gradual breakdown of central government, however, led to the Second Intermediate Period (1630–1539/1523 B.C.E.), which was dominated by West Semitic foreigners ruling in the north of Egypt while local princes of Thebes controlled the south. Egypt began to look outward with the beginning of the New Kingdom (1539–1075 B.C.E.), when a strong, wealthy central government held sway over the ancient northeast African and Near Eastern world. A Third Intermediate Period (1075–656 B.C.E.) followed, and foreign rulers from Libya and Nubia commanded the scene. The centralized government led by Libyans introduced the Late Period (664–332 B.C.E.), when foreign rule by Persians added to the rich mix of peoples living in Egypt. Alexander the Great's invasion resulted in the Ptolemaic Period (332–30 B.C.E.), which saw the blending of Egyptian and Greek culture. The Romans took control of Egypt in 30 B.C.E. with the defeat of the Egyptian navy of Cleopatra VII and Marc Anthony at the Battle of Actium. Rule from Rome and subsequently from the Eastern Roman Empire's capital of Byzantium officially continued until the arrival of Arab rulers in Egypt in 642 C.E.

PREHISTORIC PERIOD
Neolithic Period; Omari Culture, Maadi Culture
circa 5000–4400 B.C.E.

People lived in farming settlements. Nearly nothing is known of the political system.

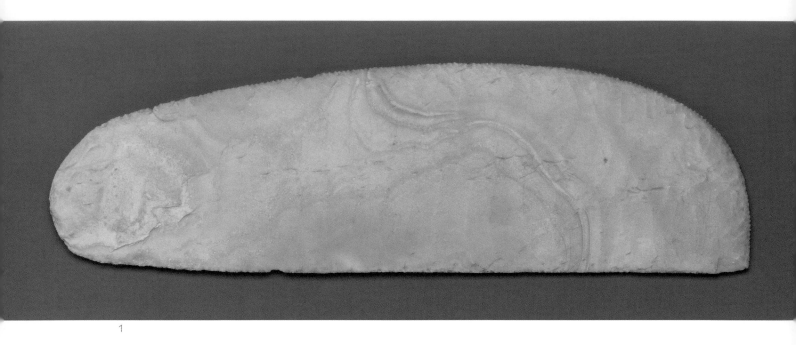

1

1. *Large Knife.* From el-Adaima, Egypt. Predynastic Period, late Naqada II Period to Naqada III Period, circa 3400–3200 B.C.E. Chert, 2 ⅜ x ¼ x 7 ⅞ in. (6 x 0.7 x 20 cm). Charles Edwin Wilbour Fund, 09.889.121

This large knife is typical of weapons included in male graves beginning in the Naqada II Period and continuing through Egyptian history.

PREDYNASTIC PERIOD
Badarian Period, Naqada Period, and Dynasty 0
circa 4400–3000 B.C.E.

The Predynastic Period witnessed the earliest villages in Egypt in prehistoric times, and it stretched to the very beginnings of recorded history in Dynasty 0 about 1,400 years later. At first, Egyptians experienced numerous localized cultures. Archaeological evidence indicates the beginnings of international trade with the Near East and Nubia and the first writing in Dynasty 0.

Badarian Period: circa 4400–3800 B.C.E.
Naqada I Period: circa 3850–3650 B.C.E.
Naqada II Period: circa 3650–3300 B.C.E.
Naqada III Period: circa 3300–3100 B.C.E.
Dynasty 0: circa 3100–3000 B.C.E.

2

EARLY DYNASTIC PERIOD

Dynasties 1 and 2

circa 3000–2675 B.C.E.

Upper and Lower Egypt (i.e., southern and northern Egypt) were unified during the First and Second Dynasties. Monumental architecture appeared in tombs, and King Narmer founded the national capital at Memphis.

Dynasty 1: circa 3000–2800 B.C.E.

Dynasty 2: circa 2800–2675 B.C.E.

2. *Shallow Saucer with Plain Horizontal Rim.* From Edfu, Egypt. Early Dynastic Period, Dynasty 1, circa 3000–2800 B.C.E. Limestone, 1 ⅛ in. (2.8 cm) high x 4 ⁵⁄₁₆ in. (11 cm) diameter. Charles Edwin Wilbour Fund, 09.889.29

The presence of saucers like this one in tombs indicates a perception that food containers would be needed in the next world.

3. *Fragmentary Ointment Jar Inscribed for Unas.* From Egypt. Old Kingdom, late Dynasty 5, circa 2371–2350 B.C.E. Alabaster, 3 5/16 in. (8.4 cm) high x 3 1/2 in. (8.9 cm) diameter. Charles Edwin Wilbour Fund, 37.76E

Royal grave goods were frequently made from the finest materials and inscribed with the king's name.

3

OLD KINGDOM
Dynasties 3 through 6
circa 2675–2170 B.C.E.

The Old Kingdom witnessed the centralization of political power in Memphis, the national capital. King Djoser completed construction of history's first stone buildings, at Saqqara. The peak of this centralized power came in the reigns of Khufu, Khafre, and Menkaure, Fourth Dynasty kings who built their pyramids at Giza. Fifth and Sixth Dynasty kings allowed power to devolve gradually to the provinces, resulting in a new period of localized political control.

Dynasty 3: circa 2675–2625 B.C.E.
Dynasty 4: circa 2625–2500 B.C.E.
Dynasty 5: circa 2500–2350 B.C.E.
Dynasty 6: circa 2350–2170 B.C.E.

FIRST INTERMEDIATE PERIOD
Dynasty 7 through first half of Dynasty 11
circa 2170–2008 B.C.E.

The First Intermediate Period included the last years of the Memphis royal house and the rise of rival kings of the Ninth and Tenth Dynasties in Herakleopolis, southwest of modern Cairo, and of the Eleventh Dynasty in Thebes. Local control was stronger than central government influence.

Dynasty 7 and 8: circa 2170–2130 B.C.E.
Dynasty 9 and 10: circa 2130–1980 B.C.E.
First half of Dynasty 11: circa 2081–2008 B.C.E.

4. *Stela of Djefi and Ankh[en]es-ites.* From Girga, Egypt. First Intermediate Period, circa 2170–2008 B.C.E. Limestone, painted, 15 ⅞ x 21 ⅜ x 4 ⅛ in. (40.4 x 54.3 x 10.5 cm). Charles Edwin Wilbour Fund, 69.74.1

Tombs in this period contained stelae (upright stones with inscriptions) in some areas but regularly omitted them in other areas.

5. *Statue of Ipepy.* From Faiyum, Egypt. Middle Kingdom to Second Intermediate Period, late Dynasty 12 to early Dynasty 13, circa 1870–1750 B.C.E. Quartzite, limestone; base: 5 ¾ x 9 x 12 ¾ in. (14.6 x 22.9 x 32.4 cm); figure: 6 ½ x 3 ¼ x 4 ½ in. (16.5 x 8.3 x 11.4 cm). Charles Edwin Wilbour Fund, 57.140a–b

Quartzite was much more rare and more expensive than limestone. In order to save money, this fine quartzite statue was set in a well-carved base of less expensive limestone.

5

MIDDLE KINGDOM

Latter half of Dynasty 11 through Dynasty 13
circa 2008–after 1630 B.C.E.

The Middle Kingdom was a period of high achievement in the arts, architecture, and letters. In the Eleventh Dynasty, political power remained in Thebes, the home of the ruling dynasty. In the Twelfth Dynasty, the seat of power shifted northward to Lisht, located southwest of modern Cairo. The Twelfth Dynasty was the apex of centralized power in the Middle Kingdom. The Thirteenth Dynasty witnessed the gradual infiltration of West Semitic–speaking peoples into the eastern delta of the Nile and increased local control.

Latter half of Dynasty 11: circa 2008–1938 B.C.E.
Dynasty 12: circa 1938–1759 B.C.E.
Dynasty 13: circa 1759–after 1630 B.C.E.

6. *Figurine of a Female.* From Egypt. Hyksos Period to Second Intermediate Period, circa 1630–1539 B.C.E. Terracotta, 4 ¾ x 1 ⁷⁄₁₆ x ⁹⁄₁₆ in. (12 x 3.7 x 1.5 cm). Charles Edwin Wilbour Fund, 77.49

Such highly stylized figurines were buried in both Hyksos and Egyptian tombs. They were likely intended to ensure fertility and thus rebirth in the tomb.

6

SECOND INTERMEDIATE PERIOD
Dynasties 14 through 17
1630–1539/1523 B.C.E.

Northern Egypt was dominated by western Semites, called Hyksos from the Egyptian words meaning "Rulers of Foreign Lands." Native Theban princes ruled the south. Most of these dynasties overlap with each other in time.

Dynasty 14: uncertain but contemporaneous with late Dynasty 13
Dynasty 15: 1630–1523 B.C.E.
Dynasty 16: 1630–1523 B.C.E.
Dynasty 17: 1630–1539 B.C.E.

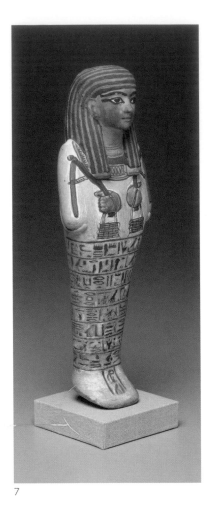

7

NEW KINGDOM
Dynasties 18 through 20
circa 1539–1075 B.C.E.

Theban princes reasserted control over all of Egypt, founding the Eighteenth Dynasty. Pursuit of the defeated Hyksos rulers into the Near East resulted in long-term Egyptian interest in dominating the area. Further expansion of Egyptian borders also occurred southward in Africa into modern-day Sudan. Kings grew rich and patronized vast architectural and artistic projects. For seventeen years near the end of the dynasty, a religious revolutionary and king named Akhenaten, together with his wife Nefertiti, worshipped only the sun disk, which they called the Aten. This brief time span is called the Amarna Period.

After restoration of religious traditions, the Eighteenth Dynasty family was replaced by the Nineteenth and Twentieth Dynasty family of kings called Ramesses. These kings maintained foreign possessions until the invasion of foreigners known as Sea Peoples. Egypt might have then lost its foreign possessions. The priests of Amun ruled southern Egypt.

Dynasty 18: circa 1539–1295/1292 B.C.E.
Dynasty 19: circa 1292–1190 B.C.E.
Dynasty 20: circa 1190–1075 B.C.E.

7. *Shabty of Amunemhat* (see also page 2 for an alternate view). From Thebes, Egypt. New Kingdom, Dynasty 18, reign of Tuthmosis IV to reign of Akhenaten, circa 1400–1336 B.C.E. Limestone, painted, 10 ⅝ x 3 ⅛ x 2 in. (27 x 7.9 x 5.1 cm). Charles Edwin Wilbour Fund, 50.128

This extremely fine shabty would have been brought to the tomb in the funeral procession in order to labor for the deceased in the netherworld.

8. *Head of a Shabty of King Akhenaten.* From el-Amarna, Egypt. New Kingdom, Amarna Period, Dynasty 18, circa 1353–1336 B.C.E. Granite, 2 ¹⁵⁄₁₆ x 3 ⁷⁄₁₆ x 2 ⅞ in. (7.5 x 8.7 x 7.3 cm). Charles Edwin Wilbour Fund, 35.1866

8

THIRD INTERMEDIATE PERIOD

Dynasties 21 through 25

circa 1075–656 B.C.E.

This period witnessed overlapping local dynasties and kings of foreign origin from both Libya and Nubia. Yet the arts flourished in this era.

Dynasty 21: circa 1075–945 B.C.E.

Dynasty 22: circa 945–712 B.C.E.

Dynasty 23: circa 838–712 B.C.E.

Dynasty 24: circa 727–712 B.C.E.

Dynasty 25: circa 760–656 B.C.E.

9. *Pyramidion of a Woman* (see also figure 93 for an alternate view). From Egypt. New Kingdom to Third Intermediate Period, Dynasty 20 to Dynasty 22, circa 1185–718 B.C.E. Limestone, 8 9/16 x 8 1/16 x 5 1/8 in. (21.8 x 20.5 x 13 cm). Charles Edwin Wilbour Fund, 05.336

Small pyramids inscribed with the deceased worshipping Osiris and Re-Hor-akhty are found in Ramesside tombs and slightly later.

10

10. *Figure of Pataikos.* From Egypt. Late Period to Ptolemaic Period, Dynasty 26 or later, 664–30 B.C.E. Faience, glazed, 2 ¹⁵/₁₆ x 1 ¹¹/₁₆ x 1 in. (7.5 x 4.3 x 2.5 cm). Charles Edwin Wilbour Fund, 37.949E

Pataikos was a protective deity, perhaps a form of the dwarf-god Bes. He was also considered a son of the god of Memphis, Ptah. Fine faience figures of Pataikos like this protected the dead. Here he is flanked by Isis and Nephthys.

LATE PERIOD
Dynasties 26 through 31
664–332 B.C.E.

Though foreigners ruled the country at this time, Egyptian culture was more likely to conquer them than be conquered. Libyans and Persians alternated rule with native Egyptians, but traditional conventions continued in the arts.

Dynasty 26: 664–525 B.C.E.
Dynasty 27: 525–404 B.C.E.
Dynasty 28: 404–399 B.C.E.
Dynasty 29: 399–380 B.C.E.
Dynasty 30: 381–343 B.C.E.
Dynasty 31: 343–332 B.C.E.

PTOLEMAIC PERIOD

332–30 B.C.E.

Alexander the Great conquered Egypt in 332 B.C.E. Following his death, his general Ptolemy established a family dynasty that ruled until the death of Cleopatra VII after the Battle of Actium in 31 B.C.E. Egypt maintained a dual culture encompassing both native Egyptian and Greek elements.

Macedonian Dynasty: 332–305 B.C.E.
Ptolemaic Dynasty: 305–30 B.C.E.

11

11. *Sarcophagus Lid of Pa-di-Djehuti.* From cemetery at el-Tarmakiya, near Hardai (Kynopolis), Egypt. Ptolemaic Period, circa 305–30 B.C.E. Limestone, 80 5/16 x 22 13/16 x 13 3/8 in. (204 x 58 x 34 cm). Charles Edwin Wilbour Fund, 34.1221

12. *A Man Named Demetrios* (see also figures 16–18). From Hawara, Egypt. Roman Period, circa 95–100 C.E., Wood, encaustic, gilding, 14 11⁄16 x 8 1⁄16 x 1⁄16 in. (37.3 x 20.5 x 0.15 cm). Charles Edwin Wilbour Fund, 11.600b

Portraits like this one were executed in a Roman style but incorporated into a mummy (see figure 17).

ROMAN AND BYZANTINE PERIODS

30 B.C.E.–642 C.E.

During the early years of Roman rule the country was directly administered as the property of the emperor. In the fourth century C.E. the Roman Empire split into two halves and Egypt was part of the Eastern Roman Empire, ruled from Byzantium (modern Istanbul). Egyptians increasingly converted to Christianity and created art that reflected the influence of the new religion. Arab Muslims conquered the country in 642 C.E.

Roman Period: 30 B.C.E.–395 C.E.
Byzantine Period: 395–642 C.E.

ISLAMIC PERIOD

642 C.E. to Present

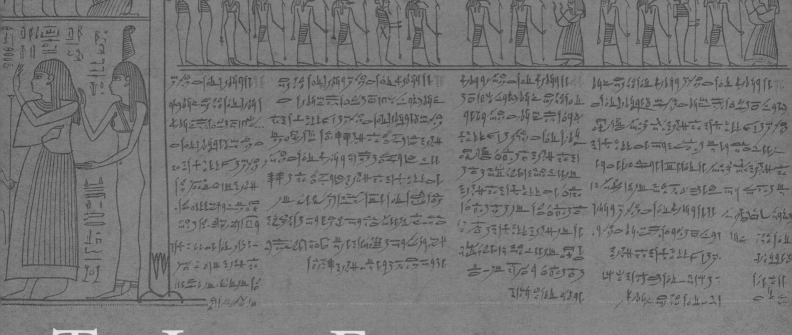

To Live Forever

Egyptian Funerary Beliefs and Practices

Edward Bleiberg

The ancient Egyptians are famous for their desire to conquer death and live forever. Kings and queens, nobles and bureaucrats, artists and farmers all shared this desire. But clearly, not everyone could afford a golden coffin, a statue made from granite or rare imported woods, or a pyramid to house them. People of lesser ranks learned to utilize cheaper materials for the same purposes (figure 13). *To Live Forever* draws on the latest scholarship and the important collection of Egyptian antiquities at the Brooklyn Museum to present a new way of looking at ancient mortuary customs. Rather than concentrating only on metaphysical beliefs about the next life, this book presents tomb objects and services as commodities, which were provided by Egyptian workshops and priests for a particular price.

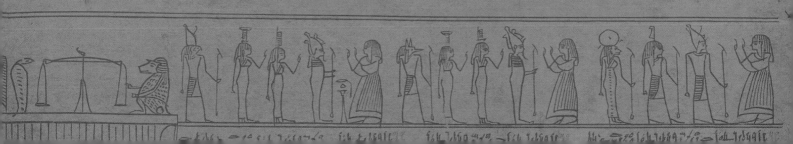

13. *Headless Statue of the Scribe Djehuti.* Thebes, Egypt. New Kingdom, early Dynasty 18, circa 1539–1390 B.C.E. Limestone, 18 x 13 x 14 in. (45.7 x 33 x 35.6 cm). Charles Edwin Wilbour Fund, 37.30E

Scribes were the backbone of the non-royal, non-noble upper rank of Egyptian society. The limestone used to make this statue of a scribe was a less precious material than granite or other hard stones.

After first summarizing the Egyptians' basic beliefs about eternity, the main text addresses the contents of a tomb, emphasizing how the process of mummification and the material objects needed for eternal life varied for members of different ranks living at different economic levels in society. And the essay contributed by Kathlyn M. Cooney, "How Much Did a Coffin Cost?," draws on her groundbreaking research to look at a specific time and place—the artists' village at Deir el-Medina in the Nineteenth and Twentieth Dynasties (1292–1075 B.C.E.)—to establish the way middle-class individuals obtained the commodities they needed to furnish their tombs. Considering these objects as items to be desired, bought, and sold reveals to us the owners' practical and financial concerns, which modern readers can share.

This book was inspired by the work of a group of scholars who have in recent decades expanded Egyptologists' knowledge of ancient funerary beliefs, practices, and material culture. They include Jan Assmann, Bob Brier, Wolfram Grajetzki, Erik Hornung, and John Taylor. Their relevant works are listed in the bibliography on pages 146–47.

Egyptian Beliefs about the Afterlife

Our first encounter with Egyptian civilization is often the image of either the pyramids, or the sphinx, or mummies. Monumental tombs and wrapped bodies represent for us the Egyptians' apparent preoccupation with death and the afterlife. Outsiders in almost every era of history have regarded the Egyptians as obsessed with the esoteric and the supernatural. From ancient Greek travelers in Egypt to the most recent American tourist, all of us respond to what we perceive as a complex and magical Egyptian belief system.

Yet the Egyptians themselves understood their massive production of objects for tombs and funerals as a purely practical response to the most basic human instinct—survival. Every object manufactured for the tomb and every ritual action performed within it was intended to ensure that an individual would survive into the next world and would then live forever. To understand the purpose of these elaborate preparations, it helps to examine the ancient Egyptian understanding of the individual's afterlife and the means the Egyptians took to ensure survival for eternity. Here it is also possible to consider how different strata of society met this need, which was felt by royalty, nobles, and workers alike, just as was the need for food, water, and shelter.

13

THE NETHERWORLD

Egyptians aspired to spend the afterlife in a region they called the *duat,* the "netherworld," whose entrance was understood to be located west of Egypt. The netherworld itself was thought to lie below the earth. Recognizing that the sun traveled for twelve hours of each day across the sky of our world until it reached the west, where it set, the Egyptians believed that the sun then spent twelve hours of the night crossing the *duat* in a boat while illuminating it. The sun is represented in a boat on coffins and in texts about the netherworld (figure 14). The sun then reemerged each morning in the east of our world. Their cosmology located the netherworld physically below this earth because that is where the sun apparently went when it sank below the horizon in the west at the end of day, until it rose in the east the next morning.

In its journey across the sky of the *duat,* the sun was threatened by the dragonlike demon called Apophis. Each of the twelve hours of the night also gave the name to a corresponding place in the netherworld reached by the sun during that time period. Apophis attacked the sun almost continuously, except during the fifth hour of the night, which was also a place corresponding to where the blessed dead were located. In some Egyptian understandings of the netherworld, the damned existed in the locations where the sun spent other hours of the night, where the continuous fight between the sun and Apophis occurred. Being present for this fight was a much less desirable place to spend eternity.

Judgment. Every potential entrant to the *duat* underwent a final test to determine whether the deceased had lived a life in accordance with the concept of justice or proper order (called *ma'at*). Passing the test meant admission to the hallowed fifth hour of the netherworld; failure meant either total obliteration or else an existence as a permanent witness to the struggle between the sun and Apophis. For the deceased, awareness in the afterlife could be limited only to the time each night when the sun was located in their one designated hour with them. The blessed deceased, however, located in the hallowed fifth hour, experienced the full twelve-hour cycle of the sun's nocturnal presence while it passed overhead in the sun boat.

Life in the Netherworld. Once the soul of the blessed deceased entered the *duat,* he or she came into a place that resembled the earthly Egypt in many ways. People maintained the same rank in the netherworld as they had on

14

earth, and thus they worked in order to receive food, clothing, and shelter. In the next world, however, the work they were required to do could be assigned to magical servant figures, called *shabties* (figure 97). Perhaps not surprisingly, those who could afford it made certain that their tombs contained one *shabty* for every day of the year so that a different *shabty* would perform daily tasks each day.

People also required food in the netherworld. Though some paintings illustrating the netherworld show fields of barley, the Egyptian's staple grain, the deceased were still dependent on food offerings from our world made at the tomb for all eternity. This was one reason why tombs of the wealthy often had farmland legally attached to them, in order to supply crops for continued offerings. Personnel, such as priests, were also assigned to the tomb, to make sure that offering rituals were performed in perpetuity.

Finally, once an Egyptian reached the *duat*, there was no further rebirth or death. This place was the final destination.

BODY AND SPIRIT AFTER DEATH

The Western tradition considers the individual to be composed of two parts: a body and a soul. This view grew from both the Greek and the Judeo-Christian perspectives. In the ancient Egyptian view, however, people were created with many more than two parts, and these elements could work in harmony or could challenge each other.

In Egyptian thought, the body itself could either be a living body, called a *khat* or an *iru;* or, after death, a *sah,* the Egyptian word for a mummy. The heart was part of the physical body, but it was additionally the organ that the Egyptians believed controlled both thought and emotion. Moreover, the heart had an independent existence after death, stemming from its knowledge of an individual's activities and thoughts during life

14. Detail of *Large Outer Sarcophagus of the Royal Prince, Count of Thebes, Pa-seba-khai-en-ipet* (see also figures 94–96). From Thebes, near Deir el-Bahri, Egypt. Third Intermediate Period, Dynasty 21, circa 1075–945 B.C.E. Wood, gessoed and painted, 37 x 30 ¼ x 83 ⅜ in. (94 x 76.8 x 211.8 cm). Charles Edwin Wilbour Fund, 08.480.1a–b

The image of the sun god crossing the netherworld is represented on this coffin below the deceased's arms. It shows the ram-headed sun god, Re, against the red disk of the sun, accompanied by the baboon-headed god Thoth. In the prow of the boat is Isis, while the ka *(soul) and wrapped* tekenu *of the deceased ride in the stern.*

27

15

on earth. Similarly, the shadow cast by an individual was an aspect of the physical, because it could be observed here on earth, yet it, too, was a separate part needing integration into a total personality after death.

Like the body, the spirit in Egyptian thought also was composed of multiple parts. The *ka* was a spiritual "double," born at the same time as the individual and represented by a statue in the tomb (figure 15). Another element, the *ba*, represented the individual's powers. Finally, the individual's name, called the *ren*, controlled the person's fate either through its use in magic or through the protection of the god invoked in the name.

In order to live forever, each of these bodily and spiritual components had to be preserved and integrated into an *akh*, or "effective spirit," that continued to eat and drink, and use tools and weapons, in the next life and could receive supernatural protection from any danger after death. Nearly every object in a tomb and every action performed for the deceased was intended to maintain the late individual's various parts as a unified *akh*.

The body in Egyptian thought was the physical container for all the other components of an individual. Its primary purpose was to act as the vehicle in which the other elements moved about the earth, used tools and weapons, and gained supernatural protection. And bodily preservation was essential to retaining these abilities in the afterlife. The preserved body not only provided a physical container for the heart and a resting place for the spiritual elements, but also gave the individual the power to be active and mobile in the next life and obtain supernatural protection. Hence the central importance of mummification, which, along with protection in a coffin and a tomb, was the physical means of preserving the body (figure 17). In addition, the recitation of the proper spells and application of the proper amulets to the mummy provided the supernatural means of preserving the body. Many of the objects found in the tomb served this same function. Yet, in Egyptian belief, the mummy itself never left the coffin, contrary to images conjured by Hollywood movies. It was the *akh*, the spiritual entity comprising all parts of an individual, that could move about the universe as needed.

The Mummy. For the ancient Egyptians, bodily preservation entailed a specific series of steps. The mummy makers' aim was to remove all moisture from the body with a naturally occurring salt called natron. This dehydration was essential to preservation. The liver, lungs, stomach, and intestines were separately preserved in canopic jars during some historical periods or wrapped separately and reinserted into the mummy during other periods.

15. *Female Head.* Provenance not known. New Kingdom, late Dynasty 18 to Dynasty 19, circa 1336–1185 B.C.E. Limestone, 5 $^{13}/_{16}$ x 4 $^{3}/_{4}$ x 3½ in. (14.8 x 12.1 x 8.9 cm). Charles Edwin Wilbour Fund, 37.268E

Statues of the deceased, located in the tomb, were one place where the ka *could rest and receive offerings from our world. This head probably came from a* ka-*statue, perhaps representing a couple that included this woman's husband.*

16. *A Man Named Demetrios.*
From Hawara, Egypt. Roman Period,
circa 95–100 C.E., Wood, encaustic,
gilding, 14 ¹¹⁄₁₆ x 8 ¹⁄₁₆ x ¹⁄₁₆ in.
(37.3 x 20.5 x 0.15 cm). Charles Edwin
Wilbour Fund, 11.600b

*Portraits like this one were executed in
a Roman style but incorporated into a
mummy (see figure 17).*

17. *The Mummy of Demetrios.*
From Hawara, Egypt. Roman Period,
circa 95–100 C.E. Painted cloth, gold,
human remains, encaustic on wood
panel, 13 ³⁄₈ x 15 ³⁄₈ x 74 ¹³⁄₁₆ in.
(34 x 39 x 190 cm). Charles Edwin
Wilbour Fund, 11.600a–b.

*The preserved body was the essential
resting place for the deceased's soul.*

16

17

18

18. Detail of *The Mummy of Demetrios* (figure 17)

Demetrios, who lived in the Roman Period in Egypt, had his name inscribed in Greek in gold letters under the winged female figure on the front of his mummy shroud, as shown in this detail. Preserving the memory of one's name in this world was essential to preserving the deceased in the netherworld and ensuring that the deceased received offerings from our world. The spelling shown here is the feminine form of the name, "Demitris," yet X-rays prove that this mummy is male. "Demitrios" is the standard spelling of the male name.

19, 20. *Heart Scarab* (front and back). From Saqqara, Egypt. Late Period, Dynasty 26, 664–525 B.C.E. Steatite and sheet gold, ⅞ x 1 ⁷⁄₁₆ x 2 ¹⁄₁₆ in. (2.3 x 3.6 x 5.3 cm). Charles Edwin Wilbour Fund, 37.717E.

The scarab beetle was the hieroglyphic sign for the word khepri, *meaning "one who becomes." It was also the name of the sun god Re at sunrise, when he came into being on the eastern horizon. The back of a scarab is a flat surface suitable for carving an inscription that would be efficacious in the afterlife. This inscription calls on the heart not to act as a witness against the deceased during the judgment in the netherworld.*

The brain was removed and discarded as unimportant. Only the heart remained attached inside the body without separate mummification. Protective amulets were placed on various parts of the body. It was then wrapped in linen bandages and put inside a coffin. The entire process usually took seventy days.

The Heart. The heart was maintained inside the body because, with its knowledge of one's life, it was needed to testify after death during the judgment period, when the individual was gaining entrance to the next world. The Egyptians regarded the heart as the organ of both the intellect and the emotions, and it was understood to be aware of all an individual's thoughts and actions while on earth. Because it was aware of a person's bad actions in life, the heart could be regarded as a possible danger to the integration of the various elements into one personality after death; therefore, a special amulet, called a heart scarab (figures 19, 20), was placed on the deceased's heart. The amulet contained ritual words that prevented the heart from acting against the best interests of the whole individual.

19, 20

21

21. *Head of a Nobleman.* Provenance not known. Old Kingdom, late Dynasty 3 to early Dynasty 4, circa 2650–2600 B.C.E. Granite, 6 ¾ x 8 ½ x 6 in. (17.1 x 21.6 x 15.2 cm). Charles Edwin Wilbour Fund, 67.5.1

After death, the individual's ka, or spiritual "double," could inhabit a statue placed in the tomb. Nobles could afford ka-statues made from hard, durable stone such as granite, as in this example.

The Shadow. The shadow also was a separate part of a person's physical manifestation. In *The Book of the Dead*, the shadow is enumerated, along with the body, the mummy, the *ka*, *ba*, and name, as an essential element combined to form an effective spirit after death. It also accompanies the *ba* into the presence of the god Osiris, king of the netherworld. Thus both the shadow and the *ba* are present when the deceased is judged. All of these elements are then available after a successful judgment to become an *akh*. In the unlikely event of an unsuccessful judgment, Ammut, the crocodile-lion-hippopotamus monster who watched the proceedings, devoured the heart. The deceased would then be truly and irrevocably dead. But such an outcome was usually avoided.

The Ka. Among an individual's spiritual components, the *ka*, or double, is the one most closely related to the physical. The *ka* and the body are born at the same time. At least for kings, the god Khnum personally fashioned both the body and the *ka* on a potter's wheel before birth. The word *ka* was also related to the Egyptian words for "conception," "bull," and "vagina," indicating its close association with the physical process of creating a new person. Moreover, elements of physical sustenance in this world are related to the word *ka*; the words for "plow," "cultivation," and even the general word for "food" are all derived from the word *ka*. Thus, though the *ka* itself has no physical manifestation, it is closely related to a person's physical self as well as to survival after death. In the tomb, the *ka* inhabited either the mummy or, more commonly, a statue of the individual sometimes called the *ka*-statue. The rich could afford to provide a hard-stone statue for the tomb that the *ka* could inhabit (figure 21). Limestone statues on a smaller scale were an economical way to provide this kind of statue to a less wealthy client (figure 76). The most common Egyptian funerary prayer, called the *hetep-di-nisu*, offered food for the *ka* of the individual. The deceased's *ka* was so mobile that it could even leave the tomb to attend rituals in the temples of the gods, if another statue was provided in the temple as a resting place. Such hard-stone statues, located in temple courtyards in the open, were available only to the rich (figure 22). When the *ka* inhabited the statue provided in a temple for this purpose, the offerings made to the god were also available to the deceased.

The Ba. The Egyptians represented the *ba*, the second major spiritual component of the individual, as a human-headed bird (figure 23). The *ba* was the manifestation of a king's power but also could refer to an individual's personality. In life, the *ba* could speak with the individual and disagree on important issues. (A text dating to the Twelfth Dynasty details a debate that a man has with his *ba* about the meaning of life on earth; the result of the debate is unclear.) After death, the *ba* could consume food and drink offerings, continue to speak and, most important, it could move. Its movements ensured continued communication between the netherworld and our world.

This travel allowed the *ba* to supply offerings made to the *ka* in the tomb from our world to the integrated personality of the deceased in the netherworld. Yet this movement also inspired discomfort in the Egyptians. They feared that the *ba* might not return to the integrated whole personality, the *akh*. If the *ba* failed to return, there would be unspecified but dangerous

consequences to the *akh*'s continued existence. *The Book of the Dead* reveals a fear that the *ba* could abandon the mummy after death, preferring to travel with the sun god Re in his solar boat rather than returning to the mummy each day as is proper. Spell 89 of *The Book of the Dead* ensures the proper return of the *ba* to the mummy, its essential resting place, and thus the eternal survival of the individual.

The Name. Preservation of the individual's name after death was indispensable to continued survival. Even on earth, the Egyptians believed, knowledge of a person's name allowed magical control over the individual. In at least one historical case, part of a criminal's punishment consisted of having his name changed, before he was executed, from Ramesu ("Re-bore-him") to Ramesdju ("Re-hates-him"). Thus even if recalled on earth after his death, his name was a continuing curse. Remembering and pronouncing the name of the deceased were so important that a variety of objects—from the tomb itself, to the coffin, to statues, to special ceramic cones in the tomb— were inscribed with that name. To ensure remembrance of the deceased's name after death, it could even be written on the front of the mummy bandages (figure 18) or on a wooden mummy label (figure 24). Sometimes, as an act of piety, sons and daughters commissioned statues or stelae (upright, inscribed pieces of stone) for their parents, inscribed with the words "in order that his/her/their name(s) might live."

22. *Block Statue of Padimahes.* Probably from Taremou (Leontopolis), Egypt. Third Intermediate Period to Late Period, late Dynasty 25 to early Dynasty 26, circa 680–650 B.C.E. Gray granite, 18 ¼ x 8 ¹¹⁄₁₆ x 8 ¹¹⁄₁₆ in. (46.3 x 22 x 22 cm). Charles Edwin Wilbour Fund, 64.146

The upraised face in this statue depicts Padimahes observing a temple procession and reveals that the statue was meant to represent him in a temple. His ka *could inhabit the statue after his death, allowing him to share in the offerings made to the god in the temple.*

23. *Image of a Ba-bird on a Footpiece from a Coffin.* From Egypt. Third Intermediate Period, Dynasty 22, circa 945–712 B.C.E. Wood and plaster, painted, 11 x 2 ¹⁄₁₆ x 12 ⁵⁄₈ in. (28 x 5.3 x 32 cm). Charles Edwin Wilbour Fund, 75.27

The Egyptians represented the ba *as a human-headed bird. This spiritual component of the deceased is capable of moving between the netherworld and the tomb or even of leaving the tomb in our world. In this example the word for "going forth" is written in hieroglyphs on both sides of the head, illustrating the close connection between the* ba *and continued agency after death.*

When the coffin of Weretwahset (her title, Lady of the House, indicates a married woman who lived in the Nineteenth Dynasty) was reused by Bensuipet (a Lady of the House and Singer of the god Amun who lived at the end of the Twentieth Dynasty), it was essential to cover the inscription on the side of the former's name, replacing it with the new owner's name (figure 126). Reused coffins are relatively common, though the precise circumstances of how a coffin returned to the market after one use are unclear. It is likely that reused coffins were considerably cheaper than newly commissioned ones.

A Proper Burial. If all the foregoing requirements were met to ensure the postmortem survival of the mummy, heart, shadow, *ka, ba,* and name, then a deceased individual was a candidate to become an *akh,* an effective spirit. These requirements all contributed toward what was called a *qerset neferet,* a "proper burial."

Yet there were additional requirements if the deceased was to survive in the netherworld. First, a tomb provided security for the mummy and the *ba.* The tomb could be built of stone in an independent building or be excavated into the side of a mountain. (Poorer people used graves in almost every period.) Also, the tomb needed a chapel with a *ka*-statue. The statue provided nourishment to the deceased by accepting the food offerings from our world. The offerings were accepted by the *ka,* which could inhabit the statue and be transported to the netherworld by the free-moving *ba.*

Finally, the perfect burial required the specialized knowledge that allowed passage through the next world and success during the final

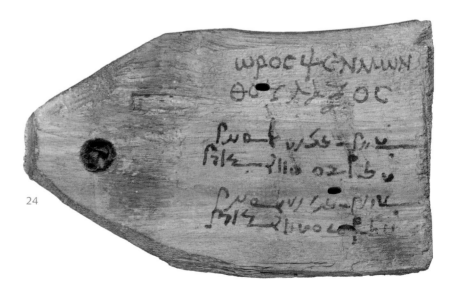

24. *Tag for Mummy of a Stonecutter, with Text in Greek and Demotic.* From Egypt. Probably Roman Period, 30 B.C.E.–365 C.E. Wood, 2 ⁷⁄₁₆ x 4 x ½ in. (6.2 x 10.2 x 1.2 cm). Charles Edwin Wilbour Fund, 37.1395E

In the Roman Period, wooden tags were used to identify the deceased, thus preserving the name.

24

25

judgment. This knowledge included the spells needed to pass through the netherworld and those needed to maintain the *akh* as a unified entity.

Ma'at. But even the most perfect physical preparations for a proper burial could not ensure survival forever if the deceased had not lived in accordance with the Egyptian concept of justice, called *ma'at*. The outlines of what was meant by *ma'at* are found in Chapter 125 of *The Book of the Dead*. The deceased recited this text as his or her heart was weighed in a balance measuring the mass of the heart against that of a feather, the hieroglyphic writing of the word *ma'at* (figure 25). The text of Chapter 125 first reviews the thirty-five negative statements the deceased should make before Osiris, here called Wennofer, among them the deceased's declaration that he or she had not killed, stolen, caused suffering among people, or offended the gods by tampering with their offerings or property. After some declarations of purity, the deceased then advanced to the forty-two guardians of the gates of the underworld, who could be represented in relief in the tomb or in paint on a *Book of the Dead* papyrus. For example, the royal scribe Yepu depicted gates four and six of the netherworld in relief on the walls of his tomb, along with the necessary spells for passing them (figure 27). As the deceased

25. Detail of *Manuscript sur papyrus.*

This scene, called the "Weighing of the Heart," illustrates Chapter 125 of The Book of the Dead. *It shows the deceased's heart weighed against the feather, the hieroglyphic writing of the word "justice" (ma'at). It summarizes the need to lead a just life in order to live forever in the netherworld.*

26. *Manuscript sur papyrus* (overleaf). From *Description de l'Égypte, ou Recueil des observations et des recherches qui ont été faites en Égypte pendant l'expédition de l'armée française,* vol. 2 (Paris: Imprimerie de C.L.F. Panckoucke, 1821–30), plate 60. Page size, 28 x 43 ½ in. (71.1 x 109.2 cm). Brooklyn Museum Libraries—Special Collections; Wilbour Library of Egyptology, EL42.1

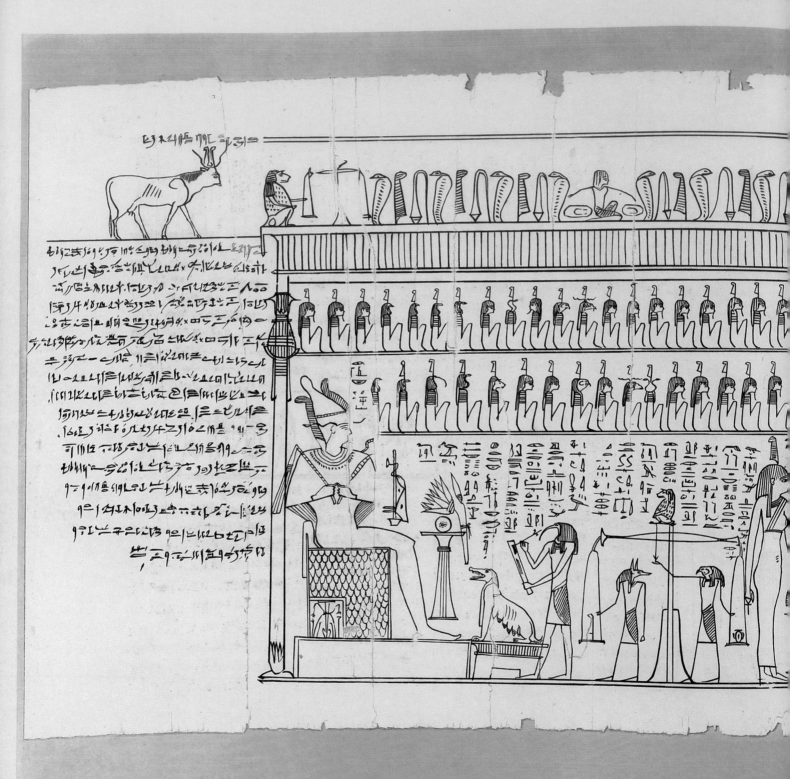

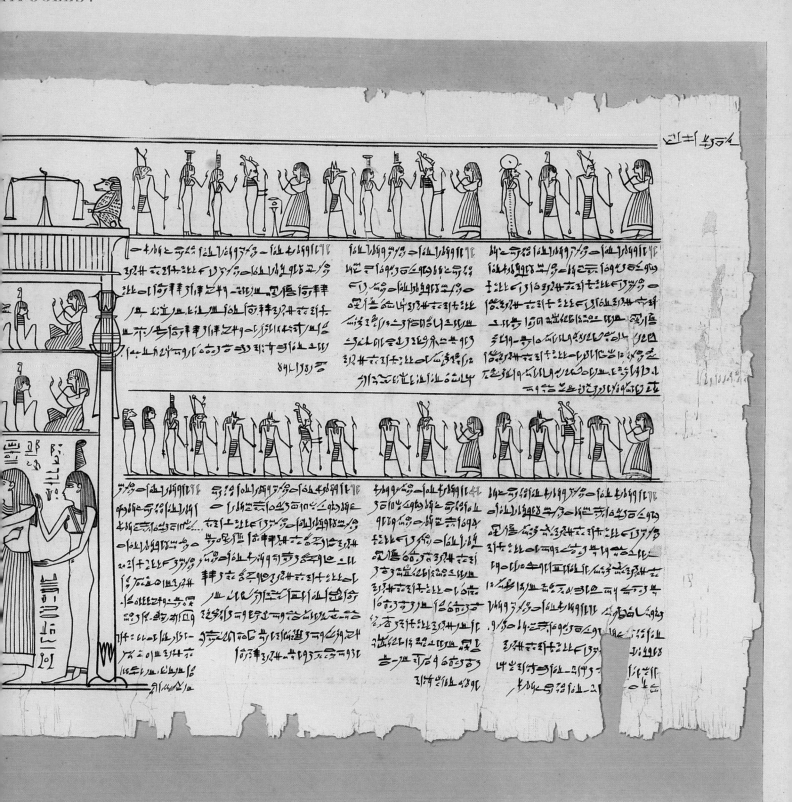

Leclerc Sc.

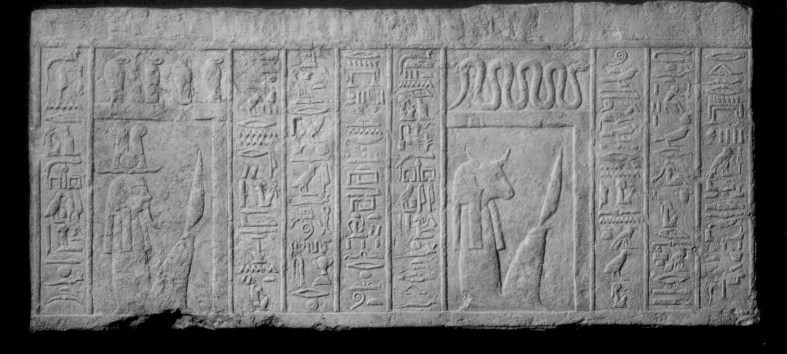

27. *Relief with Netherworld Deities.*
From Egypt. New Kingdom, late Dynasty
18 to early Dynasty 19, circa 1332–1250
B.C.E. Limestone, 10 ¾ x 24 x 2 ⅝ in.
(27.3 x 61 x 6.7 cm). Charles Edwin
Wilbour Fund, 37.1487E

This relief from a high official's tomb
represents The Book of the Dead, *Spell*
145, in which the deceased approaches
the fourth and the sixth gates of the
netherworld. The words that the
deceased should recite when
approaching them are inscribed here
along with the gates themselves and
guardian deities. The wealthier the
individual, the more this information
would be supplied to the deceased in
multiple, redundant forms: in addition
to this relief on his tomb wall, this
official likely also had a Book of the
Dead *papyrus to help him remember all*
of the spells when he reached the
netherworld. Originally these spells
would have been known only to the
king. Since the owner of this tomb was
a royal scribe and overseer of the
granary, as a literate, high official he
had earlier access to such information
than others would who did not have
royal connections.

approached each gate, he or she made a declaration of innocence regarding
a particular evil deed to the guardian deity in front of it; these denials of
wrongdoing were the deceased's opportunity to show that he or she had
lived in accordance with *ma'at.*

MYTHOLOGY OF THE AFTERLIFE

In addition to leading a good life and having a proper burial, the deceased
needed special knowledge of how to reach the netherworld. If the deceased
did not have special knowledge and therefore could not pass the test of
judgment, admission to the next world was not assured.

This specialized knowledge was based on three sets of mythological
material, originally separate, but combined by royal scholars during the New
Kingdom into a unified explanation of how this world should be ruled and
the nature of the next world. One of these myths had at its center the divine
pair Osiris (figure 28) and Isis (figure 29). The second myth dealt with the
conflict between Horus, who was the heir of Osiris; and Seth, his uncle. The
third myth concerned the sun god Re and his daily journey across this world
and nightly journey through the next world.

Osiris and Isis. Osiris and his wife, Isis, the subjects of the first myth, could
trace their ancestry back three generations to the creator of the world, Atum.
Atum's children, Shu (the god of air) and Tefnut (the goddess of moisture),
were the parents of Geb (earth) and his sister-wife Nut (sky). Geb and Nut
in turn produced four children—Isis, Osiris, Seth, and Nephthys—who

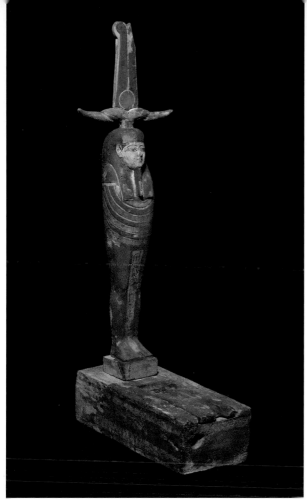

28

29

themselves later married; Osiris was paired with Isis, while Seth was the husband of Nephthys. In Egyptian, these eight gods were collectively called the *Pesdjetyu* (the Eight), known in European languages by the Greek word for eight, Ennead. They were worshipped at Heliopolis, near modern-day Cairo.

Osiris and Isis served as king and queen of Egypt at the beginning of time. According to the latest version of the myth—recorded by Plutarch (46–after 119 C.E.), the Greek historian and priest at Delphi—it was Osiris who introduced civilization to the Egyptians and later spread it to the other peoples of the earth. He taught them how to honor the gods and introduced the concept of law. Osiris used fine speech, music, and song to win over all the peoples of the earth and never had to resort to military force. He was the ideal king.

In the twenty-eighth year of Osiris' reign, his brother Seth became so jealous of the king that he plotted with seventy-two conspirators to kill him. Seth secretly measured Osiris' body and then commissioned an elaborately decorated human-form box built to his measurements, the antecedent of Egyptian coffins. When the box was complete, Seth invited Osiris to a party. In the middle of the festivities, Seth ordered that the box be brought into the room and announced that the person who fit exactly inside it would receive it as a gift. Each of the guests took a turn inside the box, but none fit exactly.

28. *Mummiform Figure of Osiris.* From Egypt. Probably Late Period, 664–332 B.C.E. Wood, painted, 24 ¹³⁄₁₆ x 4 ¹³⁄₁₆ x 11 ⅛ in. (63 x 12.3 x 28.3 cm). Charles Edwin Wilbour Fund, 37.1481E

Osiris—according to Egyptian thought, the first king of Egypt—became the king of the netherworld after his murder by his brother Seth and proper burial by his wife, Isis.

29. *Statuette of Isis.* Provenance not known. Late Period. Saite Period, Dynasty 26, 664–525 B.C.E.. Stone, 5 ½ x 1 ⅜ x 3 in. (14 x 3.5 x 7.6 cm). Gift of Evangeline Wilbour Blashfield, Theodora Wilbour, and Victor Wilbour honoring the wishes of their mother, Charlotte Beebe Wilbour, as a memorial to their father, Charles Edwin Wilbour, 16.430

Isis was wife to Osiris, the mythical first king of Egypt, and the mother of Horus (shown on her lap). Horus was thought to be incarnate in the reigning king of Egypt.

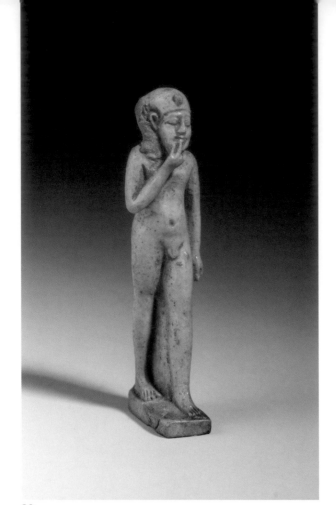

30. *Statue of Horus as a Child.* From Egypt. Late Period, Dynasty 26–30, 664–332 B.C.E. Faience, glazed, 3 ⁷⁄₈ x ¹³⁄₁₆ x 1 in. (9.8 x 2 x 2.6 cm). Charles Edwin Wilbour Fund, 37.1095E

Horus, the miraculously conceived child of Osiris and Isis, spent his childhood in the delta marshes with his mother. Later, Horus successfully challenged his uncle Seth for the throne of Egypt.

31. *Triad of Isis, the Child Horus, and Nephthys.* From Egypt. Ptolemaic Period, 305–30 B.C.E. Faience, glazed, 2 x 1 ⁷⁄₁₆ x ⁵⁄₈ in. (5.1 x 3.6 x 1.6 cm). Charles Edwin Wilbour Fund, 37.939E

Isis, now a single mother, raised her son, Horus, with the help of her sister, Nephthys.

Then it was Osiris' turn, and of course it fit him perfectly. As Osiris lay in the box, all the conspirators rushed to its side, nailed it shut, and sealed it with molten lead. Seth threw the box into the Nile, and Osiris drowned.

The news of Osiris' death was brought to Isis. She searched everywhere for the box. According to Plutarch, she finally found it in Byblos, in modern-day Lebanon, and then returned it to Egypt. Egyptian texts and reliefs suggest that after finding the deceased Osiris, Isis used magic to bring him back to life briefly so that they could conceive a child (figure 30), after which Osiris proceeded to the netherworld to become its king. Aided by her sister Nephthys, Isis secretly raised the son, Horus, born to her from this union (figure 31).

Another tradition recorded in Plutarch recounts that after Isis brought Osiris' body back from Byblos, Seth stole it, divided it into fourteen pieces, and scattered the pieces across Egypt. Isis found each of the pieces and reunited them. The individual places of discovery ultimately became the sites of the fourteen temples of Osiris throughout Egypt.

The myth continues in a New Kingdom papyrus with the story of how Horus avenged his father through a series of competitions with his uncle Seth. In one competition, Seth took the form of a hippopotamus, the symbol of chaos (figure 32). Ultimately, Horus defeated Seth and took the throne of Egypt.

32

32. *Statuette of a Standing Hippopotamus.* Provenance not known. Middle Kingdom to Second Intermediate Period, Dynasty 12 to Dynasty 17, circa 1938–1539 B.C.E. Faience (ground quartz, alkaline binder, glaze), painted, 4 ⅛ x 3 ⅛ x 7 ⅜ in. (10.5 x 7.9 x 18.8 cm). Gift of the Ernest Erickson Foundation, Inc., 86.226.2

The hippopotamus could be used to represent Seth, the god of chaos who murdered his brother Osiris and stole the throne from Horus, the rightful heir. Statuettes of hippos in Egyptian tombs always had broken legs to prevent Seth from making trouble in the tomb. These figures are typical of Middle Kingdom tombs.

The story of Osiris and Isis is important to an understanding of the afterlife in part because it forms the basis for an Egyptian funeral, with Isis and her sister Nephthys symbolizing the mourners. It is also important because it explains how Osiris, the prototype of the good and just king of Egypt, came to become the king of the netherworld, and the judge there of who was worthy to enter. As mentioned earlier, the deceased proved that he or she had led a just life during the weighing of the heart before Osiris.

The Sun God Re. At the same time that Osiris was seen as the king of the netherworld, the sun god Re held a prominent place as a creator god and also as a god of the living and the dead. Since knowing a deity's name was so integral to the deceased's achieving eternal life, the fact that Re took different forms with different names during each hour of the day or night assumed great importance. Re took three forms on earth and many more forms in the netherworld. On earth he encompassed the god Khepri at sunrise, a name meaning "one who becomes" and written in hieroglyphs with the scarab beetle sign (figures 19, 20); he was Re ("the sun") at noon; and Atum ("the completed one") at sunset. On the eastern and western horizons he was Re-Hor-akhty ("Re-Horus-of-the-Horizon") (figure 117). The text called *The Litany of Re* suggests at least seventy-five other forms, each with a different name, that the god could take during the night. The connection of Re and Atum as Re-Atum allowed Re to be a member of the Ennead without changing the number of gods included, as well as Osiris' great-grandfather. By the Fourth Dynasty, indeed, the king of Egypt was known as the "son of Re," a title that may have been viewed as originating when Osiris himself was king.

The mythological material records that Re travels across the sky during the twelve hours of the earthly day. At night, however, he spends twelve hours illuminating the netherworld, where he rides in a boat that is sometimes towed by lesser deities (figure 33). In the fifth hour of the night, Re merges with Osiris and dies. By the sixth hour, Re travels in his boat in spite of being threatened by the demon Apophis. One of Re's major defenders during the sixth hour is Seth, the same god who struggled with Horus for kingship on earth. (Perhaps this part of the myth reflects a time before the story of the struggle between Horus and Seth became part of the mythology.) Ultimately, Re enters the twelfth hour of the night, and the solar boat reaches the eastern horizon. Re then reenters the land of the living as Khepri to restart the endless cycle again. The fact that Re receives the name Khepri, meaning "one who becomes," at the beginning of the cycle stresses that in spite of the successive dangers he faces during the hours of the night, he will indeed return to the land of the living each morning.

The Diffusion of Knowledge. These three bodies of mythological material—the Osiris-Isis stories, the struggle of Horus and Seth, and the solar cycle of Re—though originally separate traditions, were coordinated at least by the time of the New Kingdom to form a complete view of life on earth and in the netherworld. In this view, Osiris was king of the netherworld; his son, Horus, was king of Egypt; and the sun god Re bound the two realms together through the twenty-four-hour cycle of his journey through them both. Yet the Egyptians themselves never recounted these stories as a continuous narrative. Rather, bits of tradition must be gleaned from three thousand years of writings beginning with what are known as the *Pyramid Texts.*

Knowledge of these disparate stories was guarded from those who had no right of access to them. Such knowledge, though a key to eternal life, was not necessarily available to all people in all periods of history. It became more widespread only gradually. The slow diffusion of this knowledge over time reveals how social rank influenced access to the netherworld.

THE DEMOCRATIZATION OF THE NETHERWORLD

The spread of specialized knowledge of the netherworld is one way that differences in rank become an obvious feature of Egyptian burials. There is a clear pattern of expansion from the top down to other ranks over time. The texts originally formulated to help kings and other members of the royal

33

family to live forever gradually became available to a wider group of people. As a particular set of spells became more broadly available, further research into the nature of the netherworld came to be utilized by kings. Later, this erudition, too, became available to a wider group of people.

This phenomenon, which the Egyptologist James Breasted called the "democratization of the netherworld," occurred at least twice in Egypt's long history. The first phase included the royal texts of the Old Kingdom becoming available to the other ranks of society during the Middle and New Kingdoms. The second phase of democratization occurred when royal texts available to kings of the New Kingdom were utilized by other ranks of society as early as the Twenty-first Dynasty.

Multiple Copies. These texts were quite important to the Egyptians. To ensure that the deceased was equipped with the knowledge necessary to reach judgment and survive it, texts of various kinds were inscribed on the tomb walls, on the coffin, on amulets wrapped in the mummy, on the mummy bandages, or on papyrus either wrapped in the mummy or in or near the coffin inside a statue of the god Ptah-Soker-Osiris. The owner of the tomb from which figure 27 came, the royal scribe Yepu, had these spells for passing gates four and six of the netherworld carved in his tomb; formerly this kind of information was available only to kings.

In general, these texts were called *se-akhu*, or "what causes one to become an *akh*." The oldest of these spells were the *Pyramid Texts*, carved on

33. *Sheet from a Book of the Dead.* From Thebes, Egypt. Third Intermediate Period, Dynasty 21, circa 1075–945 B.C.E. Papyrus, pigment, 9 ½ x 20 in. (24.1 x 50.8 cm). Charles Edwin Wilbour Fund, 37.1699Ea–b

The sun god Re rides in a boat toward his reentry into the land of the living. He is reborn into this world as Khepri. This name for the god means "one who becomes" and this word is written in hieroglyphs with the scarab beetle sign. Knowing all the names of the sun god helped the deceased gain eternal life.

the interior walls of the pyramids of kings in the late Fifth and the Sixth Dynasties of the Old Kingdom. By the Middle Kingdom, people of a wider variety of ranks had access to specialized texts, recorded on their coffins. These included the collection of spells called the *Coffin Texts*, as well as the map of the next world called the *Book of the Two Ways*, which records the paths around dangerous mounds and fiery lakes occupied by hostile forces that could block the way to the netherworld.

In the New Kingdom, the contents of the *Pyramid Texts* and *Coffin Texts* became available to the middle ranks of society through recording on their coffins (figure 34) and *The Book of the Dead* (figure 116). The older material thus became less exclusive, though kings never completely abandoned the most important spells from this group. But perhaps this democratization of the earlier texts explains why royal special knowledge was enhanced with

even more advanced and detailed research on the next world. New texts with their illustrations became available to royalty; they are generally known as *The Books of the Netherworld* (figure 35). Rather than being collections of spells, as were previously devised texts for achieving eternal life, *The Books of the Netherworld* describe and illustrate the course the sun takes while illuminating the world of the dead during the twelve hours of the night. These texts and illustrations remained mostly restricted to kings from the early Eighteenth Dynasty until the Twenty-first Dynasty. Even queens did not have the use of all of these books in their tombs in the earlier period.

Scholars divide *The Books of the Netherworld* into two groups. Two of the earlier books, written during the Eighteenth Dynasty, are the *Amduat* and *The Book of Gates*, which form one group. There are nine other known books introduced between the early New Kingdom and the Ramesside

34. *Anthropoid Coffin of the Servant of the Great Place, Teti* (see also figure 114). From Thebes, Egypt. New Kingdom, mid- to late Dynasty 18, circa 1339–1307 B.C.E. Wood, painted, 33 ¼ x 18 ¹³⁄₁₆ x 81 ½ in. (84.5 x 47.8 x 207 cm). Charles Edwin Wilbour Fund, 37.14E

An Egyptian coffin was thought to copy the human-form box that Seth used to trick his brother Osiris in the myth: by luring Osiris into the box, Seth was able to trap and drown him. The words of The Book of the Dead, *Spell 151, are included on the side of the coffin of Teti: here, from right to left, the human-headed god Hapi, the jackal-headed god Anubis, the human-headed god Kebehsenuef, and the ibis-headed god Thoth recite the spells for protecting Teti's body.*

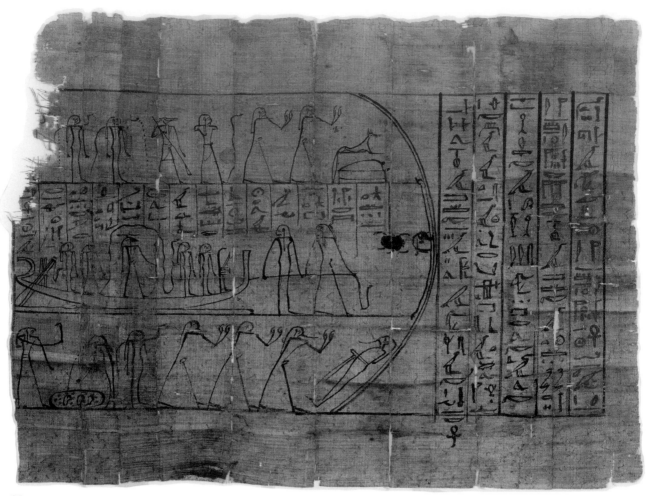

35

35. *Sheet from an* Amduat: *What Is in the Netherworld.* From Thebes, Egypt. Third Intermediate Period, Dynasty 21,1075–945 B.C.E. Papyrus, ink, 8 ⅞ x 11 ¹³⁄₁₆ in. (22.5 x 30 cm). Charles Edwin Wilbour Fund, 37.1826Ea–b

This section of the Amduat *on papyrus belonged to a priest living in the Twenty-first Dynasty. When this text was first composed, in the early Eighteenth Dynasty, it was recorded only on the walls of kings' tombs. Papyri like this were made in limited quantities for non-royal individuals beginning four or five hundred years after their original composition.*

period. Though all of them dealt with the fusion of the sun god Re with the king of the dead, Osiris, there are significant differences in their details.

Second Phase. The diffusion of the *Amduat* is typical of the way the second phase of democratization occurred. Beginning in the reign of either Thutmose I (1493–1479 B.C.E.) or his daughter Hatshepsut (1478–1458 B.C.E.), this text was included in the royal tomb and continued in use through the Ramesside period. At the end of the New Kingdom, after 1075 B.C.E., the text began to appear in the tombs of priests of the god Amun in Thebes. They inscribed it both on their coffins and on papyri included in their tombs. Then, in the Twenty-sixth Dynasty, nearly three hundred years later, the same text was recorded on tomb walls belonging to other government officials. The texts also appear on non-royal sarcophagi of the Thirtieth Dynasty and the Ptolemaic Period belonging to wealthy individuals.

The *Amduat* gives a detailed description, with illustrations, of the course the sun takes during its twelve hours in the netherworld (figure 35). It shows how the sun travels in a boat while under attack from enemies who try to prevent the sun from returning to the world of the living in the morning. The god Osiris is included, but in this text he is rather passive in the battle. The deceased, who come alive while the boat is in their realm, go back to sleep when the sun reenters the land of the living and remain sleeping until the sun returns at the end of the earthly day.

The Book of Gates might have earlier origins, but the oldest known copy dates to the reign of Horemheb (1319–1292 B.C.E.) at the end of the Eighteenth Dynasty. It continued in use by the Ramesside kings. Privately owned papyri of the Twentieth Dynasty include part of this text, as does a Twenty-first Dynasty papyrus. In the Twenty-sixth Dynasty and later, the illustrations from this book were found in private tombs. The Book of Gates also illustrates the twelve hours of night, but it reduces the number of crew members in the boat from those found in the Amduat. It also differs from the Amduat by adding a gate at the end of each hour and by more fully incorporating Osiris.

This pattern of New Kingdom royal texts reused increasingly by high officials after the Twenty-first Dynasty is also clear in The Book of Caverns, The Book of the Earth, The Book of the Night, The Book of the Day, and The Book of Nut. A variant pattern of democratization occurs, however, with The Litany of Re. Like the Amduat, The Litany of Re first survives from early in the Eighteenth Dynasty. It is found in the tomb of Thutmose III (1479–1425 B.C.E.). However, it is also simultaneously used by the king's prime minister, Useramun. The next appearance of the text in a royal tomb is in the reign of Sety I (1290–1279 B.C.E.) in the Nineteenth Dynasty. It then becomes a standard royal text. Yet the same text had already spread to officials, becoming Spells 127 and 180 of The Book of the Dead before the end of the Eighteenth Dynasty. This text, which invokes the seventy-five names of the god Re and is specially devoted to uniting Re and Osiris, continued among high officials in the Twenty-first Dynasty.

Permanently Restricted Texts. Some royal texts never became available to non-royal people. This group includes The Enigmatic Book of the Netherworld, a unique text used only by Tutankhamun (1332–1322 B.C.E.). A similar case is found with The Book of the Heavenly Cow. It also is first known from the tomb of Tutankhamun, but it continued to be used by kings into Ramesside times. There are no known non-royal copies of the text.

Finally, The Book of Traversing Eternity appears to be an original Ptolemaic text used by high officials but never by kings. This text gives the deceased access to festivals of the gods on earth.

36. *Sarcophagus Lid for Pa-di-Inpw.* From cemetery at el-Tarmakiya, near Hardai (Kynopolis), Egypt. Ptolemaic Period, circa 305–30 B.C.E. Limestone, 82 ¹¹⁄₁₆ x 28 ¾ x 12 ⅝ in. (210 x 73 x 32 cm). Charles Edwin Wilbour Fund, 34.1222

Elaborate stone sarcophaghi were available only to the very richest Egyptians. Others made do with local wood, terracotta, or even wickerwork.

36

Knowledge was thus an important element in reaching eternal life. With the right physical preparations of the body, the tomb and its contents, proper behavior during life, and, finally, adequate specialized knowledge, an ancient Egyptian felt prepared to live forever.

Mummification and Rank

Mummification is one of the defining customs of ancient Egyptian society for people today. The practice of preserving the human body was, we believe, a quintessential feature of Egyptian life (figure 17). Yet even mummification has a history of development and was accessible to different ranks of society in different ways during different periods. Indeed Herodotus, the ancient Greek historian who visited Egypt in the mid-fifth century B.C.E., observed that there were at least three different processes of mummification, ranging from what he called the "most perfect" to the method employed by the "poorer classes." There were probably even more gradations of quality in the long history preceding his visit to Egypt.

CHOOSING A METHOD

Herodotus relates in Book II of his *Histories* that the family of the deceased typically brought the body to professional embalmers for mummification, a scene often recorded in tombs as part of the funeral itself. The embalmers would show the family wooden models of corpses, painted to resemble the three possible states of preservation that could be achieved. Once the family members decided what they could afford, or what they were willing to spend on this process, they paid and left the body with the embalmers.

"Most Perfect" Method. The most expensive process has often been described and can be confirmed by examination of mummies excavated in modern times. Its purpose was to preserve the body by dehydration and protect it against pests, such as insects. Almost all the actions Herodotus described serve one of these two functions.

First, the brain was removed by passing an iron hook through the nose into the cranium and retracting it by the same pathway; the gray matter was discarded. The embalmers then rinsed the skull with certain drugs that mostly cleared any residue of brain tissue and also had the effect of killing bacteria (though of course the Egyptians were unaware that it was micro-organisms that caused decay). Next, the embalmers made an incision along the flank with a sharp blade fashioned from an Ethiopian stone and removed the contents of the abdomen. Herodotus does not discuss the separate preservation of these organs and their placement either in special jars or back in the cavity, a process that was part of the most expensive embalming, according to archaeological evidence.

The abdominal cavity was then rinsed with palm wine and an infusion of crushed, fragrant herbs and spices; the cavity was then filled with spices including myrrh, cassia, and, Herodotus notes, "every other sort of spice except frankincense," also to preserve the body.

The body was further dehydrated by placing it in natron, a naturally occurring salt, for seventy days. Herodotus insists that the body did not stay in the natron longer than seventy days, and indeed modern researchers who have tried to duplicate this process find that this is the ideal length of time for it. Any shorter time and the body is not completely dehydrated; any longer, and the body is too stiff to move into position for wrapping. The embalmers then washed the body again and wrapped it with linen bandages. The bandages were covered with a gum that modern research has shown is both a waterproofing agent and an antimicrobial agent.

At this point, the body was given back to the family. These "perfect" mummies were then placed in wooden cases that were human-shaped. Richer people placed these wooden cases inside a stone sarcophagus that provided further protection (figure 36). The family placed the sarcophagus in the tomb upright against the wall, according to Herodotus.

Avoiding Expense. The second process that Herodotus describes was used by middle-class people or people who "wish to avoid expense." In this method, an oil derived from cedar trees was injected with a syringe into the abdomen. A rectal plug prevented the oil from escaping. This oil probably had the dual purpose of liquefying the internal organs, as Herodotus explains, but also of disinfecting the abdominal cavity, as modern scientists have discovered. (By liquefying the internal organs, the family avoided the expense of canopic jars and separate preservation.) The body was then placed in natron for seventy days. At the end of that time, the body was removed from the natron, and the cedar oil, now containing the liquefied internal organs, was drained through the rectum. With the body both dehydrated and, as we now understand, disinfected and free of insects, it could be returned to the family. Herodotus does not describe the burial of such mummies, but they were perhaps placed in a shaft tomb of the type known from archaeology to have existed throughout Egypt in most time periods. Poorer people used coffins fashioned from terracotta (figure 37).

37

37. *Lid from a Sarcophagus.* From Gebel Silsilis, Egypt. New Kingdom, Ramesside Period, Dynasty 19 to Dynasty 20, circa 1292–1075 B.C.E. Terracotta, painted, 25 x 16 ½ x 7 ¾ in. (63.5 x 41.9 x 19.7 cm). Charles Edwin Wilbour Fund, 37.1518E

This mold-made, terracotta sarcophagus lid is painted yellow to imitate royal gold coffins. The same yellow was used to paint wooden coffins for the same reason. This coffin is one of a small number of high-quality terracotta sarcophagi following an upper-rank style.

Inexpensive Method. The third and least-expensive method the embalmers offered was to clear the intestines with an unnamed liquid, injected as an enema. The body was then placed in natron for seventy days and returned to the family. Herodotus gives no further details.

CHANGES IN MUMMIFICATION

Much of Herodotus' description can be confirmed through examination of mummies excavated by archaeologists. Yet Herodotus was writing about mummification near the end of Egyptian history. The beginnings of mummification are more complex than he or his informers knew.

Earliest Times. During the Prehistoric and Predynastic Periods (see "A Brief Chronology of Ancient Egypt," page 10), the Egyptians buried their dead directly in the desert sand. The sand itself acted to dehydrate the body, and such naturally occurring preservation perhaps led the Egyptians to the belief that bodily preservation was natural and necessary. Once the dead began to be buried inside mud-brick and, later, stone-built tombs at the beginning of the Early Dynastic Period, there was no sand in the tomb to dehydrate the body. Thus artificial means for preserving it were developed. This process must have developed over several hundred years. In 2007, scholars discovered the earliest evidence of mummification now known, in the form of resin-soaked mummy bandages excavated at a Badarian Period cemetery, possibly dating as early as 4400 B.C.E. Further early evidence was discovered in a multiple burial in the Abu Sir area, west of modern Cairo, dating to the Second Dynasty. One body in this shaft tomb was found (in a coffin) wrapped in linen that bore the traces of resin stains, circumstantial evidence perhaps pointing to the earliest known mummy. The linen was found under the head of a contracted body, placed in the coffin with two other contracted bodies. (In this respect, the bodies were treated more in the manner of Predynastic burials, rather than like the extended bodies known to have been mummified later in Egyptian history.) These three individuals shared a limestone offering table. But little else of their burial was preserved, making it difficult to evaluate their rank in society.

First Mummies. No such problem of evaluation attends what is considered the oldest known mummy. Discovered at Meidum, south of Giza, in 1892, the mummy of Prince Rahotep—a brother of King Khufu (2585–2560 B.C.E.), builder of the Great Pyramid—belonged to a man near the very top of

Egyptian society. Another mummy of roughly the same period belonged to Khufu's mother, Queen Hetepheres. She was the wife of King Huni (died 2625 B.C.E.), but was buried next to her son's pyramid in Giza. Her burial contained the earliest known canopic chest, a container for the mummified internal organs. When it was discovered in 1927, the packets containing the internal organs were still intact, yet no body was found in the sarcophagus. The next-oldest known mummies belonged to high royal officials of the Fifth Dynasty. Rawer II was a royal official living at the same time as Scnedjem-ib Yenty, a royal architect, both serving King Djedkare-Issesy (2415–2371 B.C.E.).

The number of known Old Kingdom mummies is not large enough to argue that these examples reflect a broader picture. But of existing mummies, only members of the royal family are known in the Fourth Dynasty, and mummified individuals among the nobility are known in the Fifth Dynasty. Perhaps the only safe generalization for this period is that only the highest-ranking members of society had access to artificial mummification during the Old Kingdom.

Middle Kingdom Mummies. In the Middle Kingdom, mummification was more widespread than in the Old Kingdom, but the surviving examples seem to have been less successful than the older mummies. Scholars suspect that full dehydration was not reached in this period because the final coating of resin was applied very thinly. The reduction in the amount of resin used was perhaps related to increased difficulty in obtaining the cedar wood necessary to make it. The cedar came from Lebanon, and in the Eleventh Dynasty even kings seem to have had difficulty obtaining enough of it to make thick coatings on their mummies and those of their families. Many of the mummies from this period are less than fully preserved.

Perhaps in a search for more thorough dehydration, in the absence of adequate cedar-resin supplies, embalmers in the Middle Kingdom began the process of removing the brain from the skull, a technique called excerebration. Some mummies from this period exhibit the nasal method of entry to the skull described by Herodotus more than a thousand years later. Other mummies reveal evidence of entry through the orbital socket of the eye or through the base of the skull. Middle Kingdom mummies often show fragmentary remains of brain matter and linen packing inside the cranium. This linen, impregnated with resin, probably eliminated bacteria, fungi, viruses, and parasites from the body. Though the Egyptians were probably unaware of the details of these possible causes for deterioration of the body, they did understand that the results of preservation attempts were better when they used resin inside the body.

38

38. *Farmers.* Detail of *Bas-reliefs et peintures de divers hypogées.* From *Description de l'Égypte,* vol. 4, plate 65, 2

Farmers, though members of the lowest rank, could effectively preserve their bodies by burial in the sand. The farmers depicted here harvest grain and prepare the soil for the next crop.

39. *Mummy of a Dog (or Canine Animal) Wrapped in Linen with Elaborate Head Molded in the Shape of Dog Head with Painted Details.* From Egypt. Ptolemaic Period to Roman Period, 305 B.C.E.–395 C.E. Animal remains, linen, painted, 18 x 7 x 3 ¼ in. (45.7 x 17.8 x 8.3 cm). Museum Collection Fund, 05.308

Animal mummies such as this dog were votive offerings for the gods. Improvements in preservation technology for human mummies also benefited the mummies of animals made in the Ptolemaic Period, which worshippers presented as a mark of respect for a god.

No Middle Kingdom mummy known today shows evidence of the flank incision discussed by Herodotus. But scholars have suggested that the method of extracting the internal organs through the rectum, described by Herodotus, was already known.

New Kingdom Mummies. During the New Kingdom, methods of mummification improved and availability became more widespread. The royal mummies of this period show the introduction of the flank incision for accessing the abdominal cavity. This approach allowed more thorough evisceration and thus more thorough dehydration of the body. The recipe of ingredients that formed the resins used to preserve the body also became more complex and more effective during this time. Natural skin color could now be maintained while still effectively dehydrating and waterproofing the corpse. Yet the majority of even the royal mummies were quite shrunken. In an apparent attempt to return King Amenhotep III (1390–1353 B.C.E.) to his natural plumpness, the embalmers tried packing linen and sawdust under the skin. Poor people (figure 38), in contrast, were still buried in shaft graves. Perhaps ironically, they could achieve equal success in preservation with natural mummification in the sand.

Third Intermediate Period Mummies. In the Third Intermediate Period, further experiments with packing linen, sawdust, earth, sand, and butter under the skin yielded more natural-looking mummies, for those who could afford this time-consuming and difficult process. It was during this time that the practical use of canopic jars to store the internal organs was briefly abandoned. The internal organs were now mummified with natron, wrapped in linen, and then returned to the thoracic and abdominal cavities. Nevertheless, dummy canopic jars continued to be placed in the tomb (figure 56).

Elaborate measures to make the body appear more lifelike were introduced in the Third Intermediate Period. They included artificial eyes inserted into the orbits. Depending on the means available to the deceased, these eyes could be made from stones such as travertine or limestone, or from bone or even linen. Ocher, a naturally occurring pigment, was now spread over the body at the end of the mummification process. Red ocher could be used to cover men's bodies, while women's mummies received yellow ocher. Though the ocher probably acted as an additional preservative, the color symbolism reveals that the ocher also had a religious dimension: the red ocher associated the deceased male with the sun god Re, while the yellow ocher associated a deceased female with the goddess Hathor, whose skin was gold. These practices continued into the subsequent periods. Again, such innovations were available only to the embalmers' wealthiest clients.

Late Period to Byzantine Period Mummies. In the Late Period, packing under the skin was abandoned. The linen packets of internal organs were now placed between the legs in the coffin or, once again, in specially made canopic jars.

During the Ptolemaic Period, when Greek-speaking kings and queens ruled Egypt, mummification was adopted by many Greek immigrants as well as continued by the indigenous Egyptian people. Additional innovations were made to preserve the body by the inclusion inside the corpse of linen soaked in resin, mud, broken pottery, and molten resins. Sometimes there was no evisceration or excerebration. The use of molten resin often trapped insects, such as beetles and maggots, that had already begun to attack the body.

It was also in the Ptolemaic Period that the Egyptians applied advances in mummification technology to the animals used as votive offerings for the gods. Dogs (figure 39), cats, crocodiles, ibises, and hawks were all preserved as gifts presented to the gods during worship.

When Rome ruled Egypt, many mummies relied on a very thick coating of resin both for its waterproofing and other preservative properties. Though the wealthy could cover such mummies with elaborately painted linen shrouds (figures 40, 41), the bodies themselves were not well preserved.

39

40. Detail of *Elaborately Painted Shroud of Neferhotep*

This naturalistic portrait of the deceased follows a Roman style of representation. Wealthy Egyptians adopted some Roman customs while preserving ancient Egyptian burial traditions.

41. *Elaborately Painted Shroud of Neferhotep, Son of Herrotiou.* From Deir el-Medina, Egypt. Roman Period, 100–225 C.E. Linen, painted, 30 x 67 in. (76.2 x 170.2 cm). Charles Edwin Wilbour Fund, 75.114

Roman Period mummy shrouds combine naturalistic portraiture with traditional Egyptian motifs including the winged scarab, crouching deities, jackal-headed birds, and a mummy on a bed.

40

41

42

Finally, Egyptian Christians of the Byzantine Period continued to practice mummification. They discontinued evisceration but used natron to dry the body. And they dressed the body in embroidered clothes, boots, and linen sheets rather than wrapping the body in linen bandages. Mummification ceased with the arrival of the Islamic religion in Egypt in 642 C.E.

The Elite Funeral

The Egyptologist Hartwig Altenmüller has divided the elite Egyptian funeral into sixteen different stages, based on paintings and reliefs in tombs of the Old, Middle, and New Kingdoms. These stages span the time from the family of the deceased delivering the corpse to the Hall of Embalming to the final ceremonies in the tomb. Though not all stages were performed for every elite funeral, this list of rituals forms the broadest catalogue of possibilities for what could be included in the funeral. The funeral was dominated by a series of processions, dances, and rituals at fixed points along a procession route all leading to rebirth into the next world (figure 43). The rituals included recitations of spells by various kinds of priests and priestesses, libations of water and milk, sacrifice and offering of animals, and formal gestures of mourning incorporated into dance (figures 50, 51). Such rituals were designed to preserve the body, feed the deceased's *ka* and *ba,* and finally to deposit the mummy in the tomb, where it could be reborn into the netherworld.

The Hall of Embalming. The first procession began as the family transported the corpse from the deceased's home to the Hall of Embalming. In the New Kingdom, professional mourning women performed ritualized hand gestures and likely sang while accompanying the body on its journey. Priests burned incense during the procession.

A second procession brought a coffin to the Hall of Embalming, depicted either as dragged on a sledge (a sled for sand) or towed in a boat on a canal

42. Detail of *Elaborately Painted Shroud of Neferhotep*

Here, on the right side of the shroud, the priests wear masks with the face of the jackal-god Anubis. The mummy rests in a boat on the hieroglyphic sign for "canal." Many of the mummy's journeys during the funeral take place either in a boat on a canal or on a sledge (a sled for sand) in the desert.

43

43. *Standing Figure of Bes.* From Deir el-Bahri, Egypt. Late Dynastic Period to Ptolemaic Period, 664–30 B.C.E. Gold, 1 9/16 x 9/16 x 3/16 in. (3.9 x 1.5 x 0.5 cm). Charles Edwin Wilbour Fund, 08.480.208

The birth god Bes played a role in rebirth, too. Thus he was included in tombs with the deceased.

44. *Relief of Offering Table.* From Saqqara, Egypt. Middle Kingdom, circa 2008–1630 B.C.E., with an inscription added in Dynasty 25, circa 760–656 B.C.E. Limestone, 20 3/4 x 16 1/2 x 1 3/4 in. (52.7 x 41.9 x 4.4 cm). Charles Edwin Wilbour Fund, 37.1355E

In this relief, the head of a bull is shown on the left side of the offering table near the hieroglyphic inscription.

(figure 49). It is likely that the coffin had been purchased by the deceased during life (as is described in Kathlyn M. Cooney's essay in this volume). The coffin procession could include priests dressed as the Souls of Pe, Sais, Hermopolis, or Hutwerihu, who ride on a sledge. The priests representing these "souls" of the early kings of Egypt wore masks in the form of the falcon-god Horus and the jackal-god Anubis (figure 42). When the coffin arrived by boat at the Hall of Embalming, the boat itself was of a special type used only by gods, called a divine barque. The coffin was covered with a cloth canopy, which Egyptologists refer to as a baldachin. Sometimes the boat included a shrine in which a statue of the deceased could be stored until reaching the tomb. On the stern and prow of the boat were priests and the materials needed for mummification. (These materials are sometimes illustrated as stored on a bed; figure 112.) When these mummification materials are included, it seems likely that this procession must arrive at the Hall of Embalming at the same time as the corpse's procession there from the home.

In the inscriptions accompanying this scene, a variety of specific destinations are named in different tombs. These destinations include "the beautiful west," "near the Great One" (i.e., the deity of the necropolis), "the booth of Anubis," and "the *senet*-sanctuary in the necropolis." All of these names suggest that the location of the Hall of Embalming was, ideally, on the west bank of the Nile River in the "city of the dead." Following the arrival of this boat, the actual mummification process, lasting for seventy days (as described earlier), began. The final ritual performed on the now mummified body was made in a section of the Hall of Embalming called the Hall of Anubis.

Journey to Sais. After being placed in its coffin, the mummy was moved to the Court of Assembly to prepare for its journey to a ritual station called Sais, again undertaken in a divine barque. The priests said, "Raise yourself up, oh NN [the name of the deceased]! May you ascend to the cult barque on the steps of cooling." The priests recited other spells that aided in the transformation of the individual into a transfigured one (*akh*), as we saw earlier. At the same time, professional mourners and priests gathered at the stern and prow of the boat. They then set off on the journey to Sais (figure 49).

On the way to Sais, there was an altar where the procession paused to make offerings. This altar was often called the *wabet,* or "purified place." The offering ceremony there included professional mourners, the two other women usually identified as impersonating the goddesses Isis and Nephthys at the funeral, and lector priests, who were responsible for correctly reading

44

the ritual text out loud. In some representations, the ceremony also included dancers called the *Muu* (figure 46).

The procession then continued to the ritual station Sais, which was also the name of a town in the delta in northern Egypt. The town was the home of the goddess Neith, one of the most ancient of Egyptian goddesses, whose worship probably originated in prehistory. The ritual at the station Sais was probably related to the role of this goddess in the funeral. Here in the cult place, the priests made food offerings that included cattle for the deceased (figure 47). The coffin, still in a cult barque, was now decorated with a jackal's skin (symbol of Anubis), Neith's symbol (two bows without their arrows), and the hieroglyphic sign for the divine (an ax or flag called *netjer* in Egyptian). The lector priest stood before the statue shrine in the cult barque and recited a prayer. A second lector priest joined the procession in Sais while the *Muu* dancers (whose headgear was perhaps meant to recall the ferrymen who transported the mummy and sarcophagus in a boat) greeted the deceased. In addition to the priests, three to five men towed the cult barque when it traveled on the Great Canal. Alternatively, the coffin with its mummy could travel in a sledge on land. Professional mourning women, rather than lector priests, greeted the coffin, and the *Muu* dancers played a more prominent role.

Journey to Buto. The next stage of the funeral was a procession from the Sais cult station to the cult station called Buto. Again, Buto was the name of a town in the delta, home of the goddess Wadjet and of the Souls of Pe, spirits who represented ancient kings of Egypt. This journey to the cult station associated with the town of Buto was perhaps the most important phase of the funeral, at least in the Old Kingdom. It is the most commonly depicted scene in tomb representations of funerals. It was also, in the New Kingdom, the illustration that accompanied the first chapter of *The Book of the Dead*. Together these facts suggest that it was one of the most central events of a burial.

The journey from Sais to Buto was undertaken on a sledge or a cult barque. Rarely, the coffin was carried by a group of priests. The coffin continued to rest under a baldachin, whether on a sledge or a barque. The journey began in the river valley, where the oxen were hitched to the sledge. It ended in the necropolis in the desert. Thus Sais and Buto are the beginning and end points for the most important segment of the funeral procession. The personnel at this point in the procession included the two women impersonating the mourning goddesses Isis and Nephthys and a priest wearing an Anubis mask (see figure 42); two or three lector priests

45. *Relief of Mourners before a Tomb.* From Saqqara, Egypt. New Kingdom, Dynasty 19, circa 1295–1190 B.C.E. Limestone, 16 9/16 x 12 3/16 x 2 3/8 in. (42 x 31 x 6 cm). Charles Edwin Wilbour Fund, 37.1504E

Two professional mourners kneel before the entrance to a tomb while one stands, making ritual gestures with her arms. Professional mourning women were integral to an Egyptian funeral.

46

47

48

46. Muu *Dancers.* Detail of *Bas-reliefs de plusieurs grottes.* From *Description de l'Égypte,* vol. 1, plate 70

Muu dancers greeted the funeral procession during different sections of the funeral. They dressed in reed headgear perhaps derived from ferrymen's hats.

47. *Slaughter of Cattle.* Detail of *Bas-reliefs de plusieurs grottes.* From *Description de l'Égypte,* vol. 1, plate 70

The slaughter of cattle took place during the procession at the ritual station called Sais.

48. *Hall of the Muu.* Detail of *Bas-reliefs de plusieurs grottes.* From *Description de l'Égypte,* vol. 1, plate 70

Two Muu dancers in tall hats stand in the hall. Above them is the same hall in plan view. The hall is located next to a vegetable garden, a pool, trees, and two obelisks.

also participated in this part of the journey; professional mourning men and women also accompanied the coffin; and dignitaries and officials followed. The priests sprinkled water and milk on the coffin and burned incense as an offering. Often a priest in a long white garment also accompanied the coffin at this point (figure 118).

The Muu. The arrival at the necropolis is sometimes described in inscriptions as "Landing at the Hall of the *Muu* of the double gate of the holy district." Though some funerals included the *Muu* at earlier stages of the funeral, in the majority of funeral descriptions their participation began here. Artists represented the Hall of the *Muu* in many tombs (figure 48). It sat in a vegetable garden at the edge of the necropolis. When the procession reached the Hall of the *Muu,* the priests called for the dancers to join the procession. The captions in tomb paintings and reliefs describe this as "the coming of the *Muu.*" The *Muu* wore very distinctive clothing, including the royal kilt and crowns, made from reeds or feathers, that resembled the tall, conical crown of the king of Upper Egypt but perhaps was derived from ferrymen's hats. The dancers stood in pairs and executed a step crossing one foot over the other, with their arms raised to hip level. In some representations they seem to sing the words, "She has nodded her head." The "she" in this song is undoubtedly the Goddess of the West, who ruled the necropolis itself. Her nod indicated that the deceased had been admitted into the necropolis. The *Muu*-dance was a way of welcoming the deceased into the necropolis. Following the greeting dance, the captions continue with the words, "Pulling the dead on the sledge by young oxen."

Journey to Heliopolis. Following this reception into the necropolis, a king's procession would continue to a cult site called Heliopolis, where rituals associating him with the sun god Re would take place. This station was called the Divine Hall of Anubis. The coffin arrived there in a boat towed by

49

50

51

two to four people. In Heliopolis, offerings of cattle were made on the king's behalf. But in tombs belonging to wealthy officials, the next step was an offering ritual without the side trip to Heliopolis.

Tomb Entrance and Burial. The coffin next arrived at the entrance to the tomb. Very commonly, the mummy in its coffin was raised from the boat and placed at the tomb entrance upright or on a so-called funeral bed. Women performed mourning movements (see figure 45) while a priest held two small containers identified in the captions as *nemset*-jars. Another priest offered incense to the deceased. A priest dressed in a panther skin raised a hook to

49. *Coffin in Boat.* Detail of *Bas-reliefs et peintures de divers hypogée.* From *Description de l'Égypte,* vol. 4, plate 65, no. 4

The coffin traveled in a boat under a shrine, guarded by priests and mourners.

50, 51. *Dancers.* Details of *Bas-reliefs et fragments d'hiéroglyphes…* From *Description de l'Égypte,* vol. 5, plate 17, nos. 2 & 4

Dancers played an important role during funeral rituals. They are often depicted in scenes of funerals on tomb walls.

52

52. *Vue de l'intérieur de la grotte principale.* From *Description de l'Égypte,* vol. 1, plate 67, no.2

Ka-statues were located in a niche inside the tomb chapel.

53

53. *Pesesh-kef (Ritual Implement).* From Egypt. Predynastic Period, Naqada III Period, circa 3300–3100 B.C.E. Obsidian, 2 ⁷/₁₆ x ¼ x 6 ⁷/₁₆ in. (6.2 x 0.6 x 16.3 cm). Charles Edwin Wilbour Fund, 35.1445

A priest used this instrument to perform the ritual of the "opening of the mouth" of a mummy. This act, in Egyptian thought, allowed the process of rebirth to go forward in the tomb by reanimating the mummy.

54. *Tekenu on a Standard.* Detail of *Mummy of the Lady Gad–Seshen.* From Thebes, Egypt. Third Intermediate Period to Late Period, late Dynasty 25 to early Dynasty 26, circa 700–650 B.C.E. Linen, plaster, pigment, 64 ³/₁₆ x 14 ¹⁵/₁₆ x 12 in. (163 x 38 x 30.5 cm). Charles Edwin Wilbour Fund, 34.1223

The tekenu, *the bundle shown here wrapped with a red rope, accompanied the deceased to the tomb. It is not clear what was wrapped in the bundle, but one Egyptologist has suggested it represents the fetus to be reborn into the netherworld. Here the* tekenu *is placed on a standard, an object resembling a flagpole.*

the deceased's mouth and performed the ceremony called the "opening of the mouth," sometimes using the instrument called a *pesesh-kef* (figure 53).

Once these rites were completed, the coffin received another food offering. Priests moved the coffin back and forth between two groups of priests. The priests on the left recited over the coffin, "Words spoken by the *ka*-priest: I am the one who pulls to the south." The coffin was then taken to the right to a priest who said, "Recitation of the embalmer: I am the one who pulls to the north."

In addition to the processions of the mummy in the coffin, a figure called the *tekenu* also journeyed to the tomb on a sledge. Known from the Middle and New Kingdoms on the sledge, and on coffins in later periods (figure 54), the *tekenu* appears to be a human figure wrapped in an animal skin or a bundle wrapped in linen with a red rope. Some scholars have suggested that a priest impersonated the *tekenu* during the procession. Interpretations of its meaning are varied. While some have seen it as a vestige of human sacrifice, a more likely explanation, offered by Ann Roth, is that it represented the fetus about to be reborn into the next world. Hartwig Altenmüller suggests that it represented the bovine form of the sun god because the priest who impersonated it was also involved in the cattle-related ritual in Sais described earlier. The caption that accompanies the *tekenu* procession reads, "To the west, to the west, the land with the good life, to the land where you should be" or, more simply, "Dragging the *tekenu*."

A separate procession brought the canopic jars (figure 55), containing the deceased's internal organs, on a sledge to the tomb. Papyrus bouquets accompanied this procession. The canopic jars most likely arrived before the offering ritual at the false door described below. This procession included

55

56

55. *Canopic Jar and Lid (Depicting a Human).* From Egypt. Late Period, Dynasty 26 or later, 664–525 B.C.E. or later. Limestone, 10 7/16 in. (26.5 cm) high x 4 1/2 in. (11.4 cm) diameter. Charles Edwin Wilbour Fund, 37.896Ea–b

Canopic jars were transported to the tomb separately from the mummy during the funeral.

56. *Canopic Jar and Lid (Depicting a Jackal).* From Egypt. Late Period, Dynasty 26 or later, 664–525 B.C.E. or later. Limestone, 11 9/16 in. (29.3 cm) high x 5 1/4 in. (13.4 cm) diameter. Charles Edwin Wilbour Fund, 37.894Ea–b

Canopic jars like this one could be "dummies"—not hollowed out or useable, but instead symbolic. When included in the tomb, even though the actual internal organs might have been replaced inside the mummy after preservation, such jars were considered magical insurance for safeguarding the organs.

additional lector priests. The procession also traveled from Sais to Buto and paralleled the *tekenu* procession.

The offering ritual at the false door of the tomb (a stone model of a door inside the tomb chapel) consisted of a large number of individual rituals (figure 57). The priests gathered the mummy in its coffin, the canopic jars, and the *tekenu* before the false door of the tomb or in front of the statue of the deceased. They brought food to the tomb in their hands, transported on mats, in chests, or on a sledge. This food provided for the survival of both the *ka* and the *ba* of the deceased.

Next, bearers delivered the other furnishings of the tomb. These furnishings included statues of the deceased (figure 58), *shabties* (figure 7) and boxes packed with sistra (figure 59), scepters, furniture such as beds, headrests (figure 60), chairs, and stools, clothing, mirrors (figure 74), jewelry (figure 61), amulets, weapons, salves, oils, and flowers. The offering ended with the slaughter of cattle and a burnt offering of the beef heart and joint in the area near the tomb.

The coffin itself was then deposited in the burial chamber. According to the captions found in tomb reliefs and paintings, the coffin was now carried by nine friends, who recited or sang, "To the west, to the west, to the land of the justified, to the completion of a perfect burial." The coffin then received libations and incense. The gathered men then shouted, "The god comes! Make landing!" In the reliefs and paintings, they are labeled "The procession, accompanied by the people of the city, toward the completion of a beautiful burial."

Although the mummy in its coffin and all the tomb furnishings were now buried, the funeral was not necessarily complete at this point. Some Egyptians were able to sponsor the so-called pilgrimage to Abydos to complete the ritual. The pilgrimage was actually a statue procession to Abydos, the burial place of the god Osiris, and derived from a royal ritual.

57

57. *False-Door Stela of a Woman.* From Abydos, Egypt. First Intermediate Period to Middle Kingdom, Dynasty 7 to Dynasty 11, circa 2195–1979 B.C.E. Limestone, 25 3/16 x 15 15/16 x 4 1/2 in. (64 x 40.5 x 11.4 cm). Gift of the Ernest Erickson Foundation, Inc., 86.226.29

This sculpted "false door" reveals some of the rituals performed in front of it. In the upper center portion, the deceased sits at an offering table, reaching for reed-shaped offerings and sniffing fine unguent. On the lower left, the deceased sniffs a lotus, a flower with narcotic properties, while her son offers her a similar flower. On the lower right, the deceased's husband receives an offering from their son.

58. *Seated Statuette of Si-Hathor.* From Thebes, Egypt, Middle Kingdom, late Dynasty 12 to early Dynasty 13, circa 1818–1630 B.C.E. Limestone, painted, 10 ¼ x 6 x 7 ⅝ in. (26 x 15.2 x 19.4 cm). Charles Edwin Wilbour Fund, 37.97E

This statuette depicts the deceased with the offering prayer carved and painted on his kilt. The statuette would have been brought to the tomb as part of the funeral procession and then used as a resting place for the deceased's ka.

59. *Upper Part of Sistrum.* From Egypt. Late Period, Dynasty 26 or later, 664–525 B.C.E. or later. Faience, glazed, 8 x 1 ¹⁵⁄₁₆ x 1 ½ in. (20.3 x 5 x 3.8 cm). Charles Edwin Wilbour Fund, 37.321E

Musical instruments such as this were part of the funeral procession and were deposited in the tomb for use in the netherworld.

60. *Headrest with Two Images of the God Bes.* From Saqqara, Egypt. New Kingdom, Dynasty 18 to early Dynasty 19, circa 1539–1190 B.C.E. Wood, 7 x 11 ¼ x 3 in. (17.8 x 28.6 x 7.6 cm). Charles Edwin Wilbour Fund, 37.435E

This headrest would have been carried in the funeral procession but would also be available in the netherworld. In general this custom ceased in the Nineteenth Dynasty as Egyptians stopped using objects from everyday life in their tombs. The reasons for this change are unclear.

58

59

60

61

61. *Necklace.* From Abydos, Egypt. Middle Kingdom, circa 2008–1630 B.C.E. Faience, shell, 18 ¹¹⁄₁₆ in. (47.5 cm) long. Gift of the Egypt Exploration Society, 26.167

Jewelry was as essential in the netherworld as in our world. This simple shell necklace would have been carried to the tomb in the funeral procession to be worn in the netherworld.

62. *Relief of Khamwasemen and His Wife Seated at the Table of Offerings with Standing Priest.* From Lower Egypt. New Kingdom, Ramesside Period, Dynasty 19 to Dynasty 20, circa 1292–1075 B.C.E. Limestone, 28 ¹⁵⁄₁₆ x 42 ¹⁵⁄₁₆ x 6 ¹¹⁄₁₆ in. (73.5 x 109 x 17 cm). Charles Edwin Wilbour Fund, 37.35E

In the Ramesside Period, the deceased are often depicted eating the funeral meal with their sons and daughters in attendance. The sem priest stands to the right of the offering table and wears a panther skin.

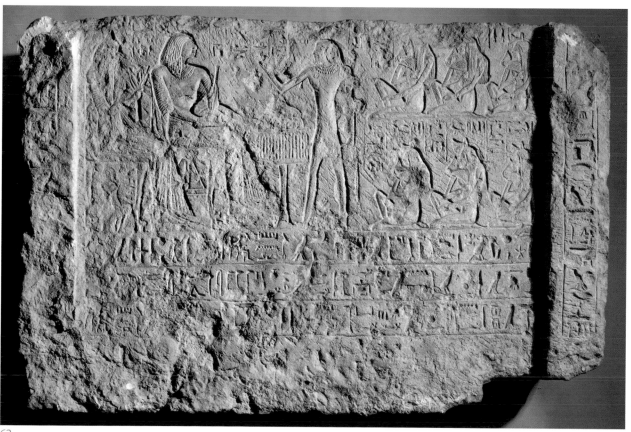

62

63

63. *Statue of a Priest, Wen-amun Son of Nes-ba-neb-dedet and Ta-sherit-Khonsu.* From Thebes, Egypt. Ptolemaic Period, circa 50 B.C.E. Limestone, 15 ³⁄₈ x 3 ¹⁄₁₆ x 7 ¹⁄₁₆ in. (39 x 7.7 x 18 cm). Charles Edwin Wilbour Fund, 36.834

Striding male statues, first known in Old Kingdom tombs, reappeared in the Ptolemaic Period. Typically they received offerings for the ka of the deceased.

It was never as important for ordinary Egyptians to participate in this ritual, though it is represented in some private tombs.

After the Burial. After the actual burial, priests performed protective rites at the door of the tomb, for most Egyptians. Using incense, four priests of different types performed this ritual. The priests included the panther-skin-clad *sem*-priest (figure 62), the lector priest, and two other specialized priests called the god's father and the *imy-khenet*. The lector read, "Rejoice together with the Westerners and extend your protection over NN when the book 'The Protection of the God Is Around Me' is read."

Priests performed the full sixteen steps in the funerals for kings and the highest officials. Poorer people had abbreviated versions of this ritual, though it is impossible to know which parts they used.

Priests also continued to perform rituals in the tomb for the deceased long after the funeral. Primary among these was the food offering ritual made before the *ka*-statue (figure 63). Egyptians described this ritual as recurring "forever and ever." The known fact that such cults were almost always eventually abandoned, however, produced a desire for ever-better security arrangements, and also some cynicism among the educated.

The dead were also memorialized in homes. They played a role in the continuing lives of their surviving relatives and were asked to settle disputes among the living. In Deir el-Medina in the Ramesside Period, both rich and poor remembered their relatives in the next world with representations of them kept at home: both the most expensive limestone busts of ancestors (figure 128) and the cheaper pottery imitations (figure 127) were displayed in homes there.

Tombs over Time: An Inventory

The traditions concerning Egyptian tombs and their contents did not spring into existence fully developed at the beginning of history. Tombs had their origins in Prehistoric and Predynastic graves and changed regularly over time in response to evolving religious ideas and political situations. This section examines the development of burial customs within the context of Egyptian history (see "A Brief Chronology of Ancient Egypt," pages 8–21), noting the introduction of new types of grave goods that then became traditional and the abandonment of old customs as practices changed. Much of what follows is descriptive rather than interpretive. Often there is little evidence other than the appearance or disappearance of a class of objects from tombs in general to suggest that changes were occurring in attitudes and beliefs.

Prehistoric Period: The Earliest Burials. The first farmers in Egypt are known from the villages of Omari and Maadi in the north. The people of these villages buried their dead in simple, round graves with one pot. The body was neither treated nor arranged in a regular way as would be the case later in the historical period. Without any written evidence, there is little to provide information about contemporaneous beliefs concerning the afterlife except for the regular inclusion of a single pot in the grave. In view of later customs, the pot was probably intended to hold food for the deceased.

Predynastic Period: The Development of Funerary Customs. Funerary customs developed during the Predynastic Period from those of the Prehistoric Period. At first people excavated round graves with one pot in the Badarian Period (4400–3800 B.C.E.), continuing the tradition of Omari and Maadi cultures (figure 64). By the end of the Predynastic Period, there were increasing numbers of objects deposited with the body in rectangular graves, and there is growing evidence of rituals practiced by Egyptians of the Naqada II Period (3650–3300 B.C.E.). At that time, bodies were regularly arranged in a crouched or fetal position with the face toward either the east (the rising sun) or the west (which in this historical period was the land of the dead). Artists painted jars with funeral processions and perhaps ritual dancing. Figures of bare-breasted women with birdlike faces and their legs

64

64. *Bowl with Lug Handles.* Provenance not known. Old Kingdom, circa 2675–2170 B.C.E. Serpentine or diorite, 1 ¹⁵⁄₁₆ in. (5 cm) high x 3 ⁹⁄₁₆ in. (9 cm) diameter. Charles Edwin Wilbour Fund, 09.889.5

Simple stone pots were a basic feature included in Egyptian graves from the very beginning and throughout their history. Such bowls originally contained food offerings for the deceased.

65   66

65. *Female Figurine.* From el-Ma'mariya, Egypt. Predynastic Period, Naqada II Period, circa 3650–3300 B.C.E. Terracotta, painted, 13 ³⁄₈ x 5 x 2 ½ in. (34 x 12.7 x 6.4 cm). Charles Edwin Wilbour Fund, 07.447.502

66. *Female Figurine.* From el-Ma'mariya, Egypt. Predynastic Period, Naqada II Period, circa 3650–3300 B.C.E. Terracotta, painted, 11 ½ x 5 ½ x 2 ½ in. (29.2 x 14 x 6.4 cm). Charles Edwin Wilbour Fund, 07.447.505

This figurine depicts a woman with a birdlike face or wearing a mask with a bird's beak. Such figures could have represented goddesses or priestesses who were part of the funeral procession.

67. *Egg-Shaped Mace Head.* From Mohamarieh, Egypt. Predynastic Period, Naqada II Period or later, circa 3500–3300 B.C.E. Alabaster, 2 ³⁄₁₆ (5.6 cm) high x 2 ³⁄₁₆ in. (5.5 cm) diameter. Charles Edwin Wilbour Fund, 09.889.198

Weapons appeared in men's graves in the Naqada II Period, the beginning of gender differences in grave goods.

67

concealed under a skirt also appeared in some graves (figures 65, 66). Some graves were much richer in goods than others, demonstrating the beginnings of social stratification. Gender differences in burials emerged with the inclusion of weapons in men's graves (figure 67) and cosmetic palettes in women's graves (figure 68). These elements were the true roots of later burial traditions in the historical periods.

Early Dynastic Period: The Use of Tombs and Coffins. By the First Dynasty, some Egyptians were wealthy enough to build tombs over their burials rather than placing their bodies in simple pit graves dug into the sand. The rectangular, mud-brick tomb with an underground burial chamber, called a mastaba, developed in this period. These tombs had niched walls, a style of building called the palace-facade motif because the walls imitated those surrounding the palace of the king. Since commoners as well as kings, however, had such tombs, the architecture suggests that in death, some wealthy people did achieve an elevated status. Later in the historical period, it is certain that the deceased was associated with the god of the dead, Osiris.

Grave goods expanded to include furniture, jewelry, and games, as well as the weapons, cosmetic palettes, and food supplies in decorated jars known

68

68. *Palette with Two Stylized Bird Heads.* From Gebelein, Egypt. Predynastic Period, late Naqada II Period to Naqada III Period, circa 3500–3100 B.C.E. Slate with shell inlay, 5 1/16 x 3/8 x 11 5/8 in. (12.9 x 1 x 29.5 cm). Gift of Evangeline Wilbour Blashfield, Theodora Wilbour, and Victor Wilbour honoring the wishes of their mother, Charlotte Beebe Wilbour, as a memorial to their father, Charles Edwin Wilbour, 16.580.126

Cosmetic palettes were used to grind galena into eye paint. They appear in women's graves at the same time that weapons begin to appear in men's graves.

earlier, in the Predynastic Period. Now, however, in the richest tombs, grave goods numbered in the thousands. Only the newly invented coffins for the body were made specifically for the tomb. (There is also some inconclusive evidence for mummification.) Other objects deposited in the tombs had been used during daily life (figure 2), suggesting that Egyptians already in the First Dynasty anticipated needing in the next world many of the same things used in this life.

Further continuity from this life to the next can be found in the positioning of tombs: those persons who served the king during their lifetimes chose burials in close proximity to their lord. The use of a stela, an upright stone with an inscription, in front of the tomb began in the First Dynasty, indicating a desire to individualize the tomb with the deceased's name.

69

69. *Swamp Scene.* From Giza, Egypt. Old Kingdom, Dynasty 5 to Dynasty 6, circa 2500–2170 B.C.E. Limestone; larger block: 14 ¹⁵/₁₆ x 25 ⁹/₁₆ x 1 ³/₁₆ in. (38 x 65 x 3 cm); smaller block: 14 ¹⁵/₁₆ x 12 ³/₁₆ x 1 ¾ in. (38 x 31 x 4.5 cm). Charles Edwin Wilbour Fund, 69.115.2a–b

Scenes of daily life in this world decorated tombs, ensuring magically that the next world would resemble this one. The swamps along the Nile, shown here, were an important food source for the Egyptians.

70. *Upper Part of a False Door of Sethew.* From Giza, Egypt. Old Kingdom, Dynasty 5, circa 2500–2350 B.C.E. Limestone, painted, 22 ¹/₁₆ x 20 ½ x 4 ¹⁵/₁₆ in. (56 x 52 x 12.5 cm). Charles Edwin Wilbour Fund, 37.34E

Offering scenes carved on the walls of tombs ensured that the offerings would continue for eternity. Thus the Egyptians could be sure that food would reach the deceased in the netherworld even if priests stopped making the offerings.

Old Kingdom: Pyramids and Mummies. In the Old Kingdom, kings first built pyramids for their own tombs surrounded by stone mastaba tombs for their high officials. The fact that most high officials were also royal relatives suggests another motivation for such placement: these complexes were also family cemeteries.

Among the elite, bodies were now mummified, wrapped in linen bandages, sometimes covered with modeled plaster, and placed in stone sarcophagi or plain wooden coffins. At the end of the Old Kingdom, mummy masks in cartonnage (linen soaked in plaster, modeled, and painted) also appeared. Canopic containers now held the internal organs. Amulets made of gold, faience, and carnelian first appeared in various shapes to protect different parts of the body. There is also the first evidence of inscriptions inside the coffins of the elite during the Old Kingdom.

Grave goods were still included underground in burial chambers, but additionally food production, scenes of daily life (figure 69), and offering scenes (figure 70) were depicted on the walls of the chapels now accessible from ground level inside the tombs. These scenes carved in relief supplemented grave goods for the deceased by making the goods depicted available through their representation.

The new false door was a non-functioning stone sculpture of a door into the tomb, found either inside the chapel or on the outside of the mastaba (see figure 57); it served as a place to make offerings and recite prayers for the deceased. Statues of the deceased were now included in

tombs and used for ritual purposes (figure 71); they were placed in a niche (see figure 52). In some elite tombs, pairs of offering stands were available to receive the offering (figure 72). By the Sixth Dynasty, some elite tombs had long hieroglyphic inscriptions, sometimes called biographies, which described the deceased's life as it conformed to *ma'at* (justice).

Burial chambers of some private people received their first decorations in addition to the decoration of the chapels. At the end of the Old Kingdom, the burial chamber decorations depicted offerings, but not people. This custom was originally restricted to royalty. Late in the Sixth Dynasty, wooden statues of the deceased were included in the burial chamber. The first wooden models of servants working also appeared in tombs at this time in elite tombs.

Some workers had small pyramids or beehive-shaped tombs reaching only three feet high with limited grave goods. Sometimes in addition to jars for food, copper mirrors could be included in women's graves. The poorest people continued to be buried in pits dug into the sand with a limited number of grave goods.

First Intermediate Period: Regional Styles. The political situation in the First Intermediate Period, with many centers of power, is clearly reflected in the many local styles of art and burial at this time. The many regional styles for decorating coffins make their origins easy to distinguish from each other. For example, some coffins have one-line inscriptions, and many styles include the depiction of *wadjet* eyes (the human eye with the markings of a falcon). There are also regional variations in the hieroglyphs used to decorate coffins. In addition, in some places tombs regularly contained wooden models and particular kinds of seals resembling buttons. And in certain locations, burials seem always to have included a stela (see figure 4), while in other locations burials always omitted them. Tombs in the Qau-Mostagedda area of Middle Egypt are notable for an unusually high concentration of gold objects.

Occasionally men had tools and weapons (figure 73) in their graves, while some women had jewelry and cosmetic objects such as mirrors (figure 74). Grindstones were sometimes included in women's tombs, perhaps to be considered a tool for food preparation in the next world, just as the weapons in men's tombs imply men's assignment to a role in fighting.

Middle Kingdom: Changing Contents of Tombs. Burial customs in the Middle Kingdom reflect some of the political trends of this period. During the Eleventh Dynasty, tombs were cut into the mountains of Thebes

71. *Seated Statue of the Superintendent of the Granary Irukaptah.* From Saqqara, Egypt. Old Kingdom, late Dynasty 5, circa 2425–2350 B.C.E. Limestone, 29 ¾ x 11 x 16 ⁹⁄₁₆ in. (75.5 x 28 x 42 cm). Charles Edwin Wilbour Fund, 37.20E

Statues of the deceased began to be placed in tombs in the Old Kingdom and became a constant feature of tomb equipment.

72. *Offering Stand of Irukaptah with Bowl.* From Saqqara, Egypt. Old Kingdom, Dynasty 5, circa 2500–2350 B.C.E. Limestone, granite, 16 ⁹⁄₁₆ (42 cm) high x 7 ⁵⁄₁₆ in. (18.5 cm) diameter. Charles Edwin Wilbour Fund, 37.18Ea–b

This offering stand and bowl were part of a pair found in this high official's tomb. They provided a place for the priest to place food offerings during the daily ritual performed for Irukaptah after his death.

72

73. *Dagger with Handle.* From Egypt.
Middle Kingdom, Dynasty 12, circa
1938–1759 B.C.E. Copper, ebony, and
ivory (?), 9 7/16 x 1 3/4 x 9/16 in. (24 x 4.5
x 1.5 cm). Charles Edwin Wilbour Fund,
05.328

*By the Middle Kingdom, the dagger was
the weapon of choice for inclusion in a
tomb, rather than the older mace.*

74. *Mirror with Handle in the Form of
a Woman.* From el-Amarna, Egypt. New
Kingdom, Amarna Period, late Dynasty
18, circa 1352–1336 B.C.E. Bronze, 6 1/8
x 5 9/16 x 1 in. (15.5 x 14.2 x 2.6 cm).
Gift of the Egypt Exploration Society,
25.886.1

*Mirrors were often deposited in
women's tombs beginning in the First
Intermediate Period. They were carried
in the funeral procession and intended
for use in the netherworld.*

73

74

surrounding the king's tomb or in local cemeteries in Upper and Middle Egypt; Thebes was the native city of the Eleventh Dynasty kings, and they preferred to be buried there (figure 75). But by the Twelfth Dynasty, high officials served the kings of a new family now ruling from the north in Lisht; these kings and their high officials preferred burial in a mastaba near the pyramids belonging to their masters. Moreover, the difference in topography between Thebes and Lisht led to a difference in tomb type: in the north, nobles built mastaba tombs on the flat desert plateau, while in the south, local dignitaries continued to excavate tombs in the mountain.

For those of ranks lower than royal courtiers during the Eleventh Dynasty, tombs were simpler. Coffins could be simple wooden boxes with the body either mummified and wrapped in linen or simply wrapped without mummification, and the addition of a cartonnage mummy mask. Some tombs included wooden shoes and a simple statue near the body. In one burial there were only twelve loaves of bread, a leg of beef, and a jar of beer for food offerings. Jewelry could be included, but only rarely were

75. *Sunk Relief of Queen Neferu.* From the tomb of Queen Neferu, Thebes (Deir el-Bahri), Egypt. Middle Kingdom, second part of Dynasty 11, reign of Mentuhotep II, circa 2008–1957 B.C.E. Limestone, painted, 7 ½ x 9 5/16 x ¾ in. (19 x 23.6 x 1.9 cm). Charles Edwin Wilbour Fund, 54.49

High-quality reliefs adorned the tomb of this queen. In this scene of daily life, a hairdresser creates a curl in the royal coiffure.

75

76

objects of great value found in non-elite graves (figure 77). Some burials continued to include the wooden models that were popular during the First Intermediate Period. They would be included in burials until about the middle of the Twelfth Dynasty. Wooden models of boats, scenes of food production, craftsmen and workshops, and professions such as scribes or soldiers have been found in tombs of this period.

The groupings of royal and high officials' tombs in the Twelfth Dynasty and in the north perhaps imitated the relationships between the tombs of Old Kingdom kings and their officials, which the rulers of the Middle Kingdom could still see and visit in their own time. Yet, unlike the Old Kingdom kings, the Middle Kingdom officials were less likely to be members of the same family as the king.

Twelfth Dynasty mastabas of court officials are less well known than the Old Kingdom mastabas because they are poorly preserved. Rather than being built from solid stone, as had been the case in the Old Kingdom, Twelfth Dynasty mastabas of courtiers were built of mud brick faced with limestone, a cheaper and quicker method. These facades mostly disappeared long ago. Yet the rare preserved examples exhibit high-quality relief sculpture (figure 44).

Those mastabas built earlier in the Twelfth Dynasty have interior rooms with some reliefs. Later mastabas have decoration on the exterior of a solid structure without rooms inside. The poor preservation of these tombs makes description of their subjects difficult. Some seem to show offering tables. Other tombs appear to be decorated with representations of wooden beams at the corners and a vaulted roof, similar to coffin decoration of the period. Some bore the palace-facade motif known from the Old Kingdom.

Some rectangular coffins of the Twelfth Dynasty have short inscriptions and representations of the most important offerings the deceased required. For men the objects depicted included weapons and symbols of office as well as food. Women's coffins depicted mirrors, sandals, and jars containing food and drink (see figure 111). Some coffins included texts that were later versions of the royal *Pyramid Texts* known from the end of the Fifth and beginning of the Sixth Dynasties. By the middle of the Twelfth Dynasty, coffins could become more elaborate. Some examples of rectangular wooden coffins contained anthropoid (human-shaped) inner coffins within them. The anthropoid coffins either depict the deceased wearing a wig or, later, the royal headcloth (*nemes*). Yet anthropoid coffins remained rare until the Eighteenth Dynasty.

Outstanding examples of the sculptor's art survive from elite tombs of the period. The earliest sculptures hark back to the styles of the Old

76. *Statuette of Sennefer.* Provenance not known. Middle Kingdom, early to mid-Dynasty 12, reign of Amunemhat I to reign of Senwosret II, circa 1938–1837 B.C.E. Limestone, painted, 6 ½ x 3 ⅛ x 4 ¹³⁄₁₆ in. (16.5 x 7.9 x 12.2 cm). Museum Collection Fund, 11.658

Small-scale limestone statues of the deceased like this one could provide a resting place for the ka just as well as expensive granite statues, at a lower cost. Here, the funerary prayer is visible inscribed on Sennefer's kilt. Middle Kingdom statuary reflected an interest in the past, as in the pose used here, which had already been in use for seven hundred years by that time, but it also reflected the deceased's present era, as in the contemporaneous hairstyle shown.

77. *Hollow Cylindrical Amulet.* From Saqqara, Egypt. Middle Kingdom, Dynasty 12, circa 1938–1759 B.C.E. Gold, amethyst, 1 ⅞ in. (4.8 cm) high x ⁵⁄₁₆ in. (0.8 cm) diameter. Charles Edwin Wilbour Fund, 37.701E

Craftsmen provided exquisitely worked amulets to protect their wealthiest clients.

77

78. *Head in Short Wig.* Provenance not known. Middle Kingdom, early Dynasty 12, reign of Amunemhat I to reign of Senwosret I, circa 1938–1875 B.C.E. Limestone, 4 ½ x 3 x 3 ½ in. (11.4 x 7.6 x 8.9 cm). Charles Edwin Wilbour Fund, 77.6

Middle Kingdom tombs included statues of the deceased. These drew on historical examples from the Old Kingdom but sometimes updated the hairstyles, as is the example here, revealing the ears.

78

Kingdom while still incorporating contemporaneous features. The short wig seen in figure 78 is an Old Kingdom style updated by revealing the ears in the Middle Kingdom manner. Though relief from these tombs is rarely preserved, the high-quality sculpture in elite tombs demonstrates the skill of Twelfth Dynasty artists.

In the Eleventh and Twelfth Dynasties, the first canopic jars containing the deceased's internal organs appeared in elite tombs. The earliest examples have stoppers modeled to resemble human heads (figure 79). By the Twelfth Dynasty, some stoppers were carved to resemble the four sons of Horus— one human-headed but the other three jar stoppers bearing the heads of a baboon, a jackal, and a falcon. This custom continued into later periods, though human-headed stoppers also remained common through the middle of the Eighteenth Dynasty. The provincial examples of canopic jars are often dummies, never hollowed out for actual use. Canopic jars are good examples of the gradual development of a custom at a royal cemetery that was

79

79. *Jar Lid with Human Face.* From Egypt. Middle Kingdom, mid-Dynasty 12, circa 1876–1837 B.C.E. Limestone, 4 x 4 ⁷⁄₁₆ x 4 ¹⁄₁₆ in. (10.2 x 11.2 x 10.3 cm). Purchased with funds given by Christos G. Bastis and the Charles Edwin Wilbour Fund, 87.78

Human-headed lids for canopic jars began to appear in the Middle Kingdom. The baboon-, jackal-, and falcon-headed lids were a later innovation.

subsequently adopted in a cheaper form in provincial cemeteries. Egyptians continued to include such jars in their tombs until late in their history.

In the mid-Twelfth Dynasty, the kinds of boat models placed in the tomb changed to incorporate divine boats, those specially used by gods, as opposed to the ordinary sailing and rowing boat models found earlier. These model divine boats sometimes contain a model of the mummy of the deceased, perhaps a reference to a pilgrimage to the sacred site of Abydos, home of the god Osiris, during the deceased's lifetime or, alternatively, a reference to the funeral procession across the Nile. As boat models such as these increased, the number of workshop and other work-related models decreased. The change perhaps reflects a greater interest in representing the funeral and a lessened concern about food production for the deceased. A similar change occurred between the Eighteenth and Nineteenth Dynasties.

Another kind of faience model of the deceased as a mummy seems to anticipate the use of *shabty* figurines (also called a *shawabty* or an *ushabty*)

80. *Senwosret III.* From Hierakonpolis, Egypt. Middle Kingdom, Dynasty 12, reign of Senwosret III, circa 1836–1818 B.C.E. Granite, 21 ⁷⁄₁₆ x 7 ½ x 13 ¹¹⁄₁₆ in. (54.5 x 19 x 34.7 cm). Charles Edwin Wilbour Fund, 52.1

Senwosret III's governmental reforms caused changes in burial customs, requiring high officials to be buried near the capital and the king's pyramid rather than in provincial centers.

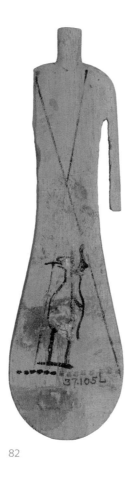

81   82

81. *Paddle Doll* (front). Provenance not known. Middle Kingdom, circa 2008–1630 B.C.E. Wood, 8 ⁵⁄₁₆ x 2 ⁷⁄₁₆ x ³⁄₁₆ in. (21.1 x 6.2 x 0.5 cm). Charles Edwin Wilbour Fund, 37.104E

Paddle dolls, highly stylized figurines of women, were placed in men's tombs and perhaps ensured fertility and thus rebirth into the next world.

82. *Paddle Doll* (back). Provenance not known. Middle Kingdom, circa 2008–1630 B.C.E. Wood, 8 ¹⁄₈ x 2 ⁵⁄₁₆ x ¼ in. (20.6 x 5.8 x 0.6 cm). Charles Edwin Wilbour Fund, 37.105E

The pregnant hippopotamus drawn on the back of this female figurine was a symbol of Taweret, the goddess who protected pregnant women. It was placed in the tomb to ensure fertility and rebirth into the netherworld. The female hippopotamus was a fertility goddess and therefore considered positive, whereas the male hippopotamus represented Seth, god of chaos, and was thus a negative force.

later in the Twelfth Dynasty. These early figurines do not have the text directing the figure to work in the place of the deceased that is found on later figurines. The richest people had stone figurines that seem to anticipate *shabties*, though some scholars have seen them as mummy substitutes rather than servant figures. Jewelry continued to be included in tombs.

Burials of the poor in the early Twelfth Dynasty changed little from those of their ancestors in the Eleventh Dynasty or, even earlier, in the First Intermediate Period. A few vessels and perhaps some jewelry, including scarabs, were included in shallow shafts. Some poorer people had coffins made of mud brick rather than only wrapping the body in linen. In one cemetery in Upper Egypt, poor people had terracotta models of houses in their shaft tombs; perhaps these models substituted for a mastaba in the eyes of their owners.

In the later Twelfth Dynasty, significant changes occurred in burials, perhaps reflecting administrative changes enacted by King Senwosret III (1836–1818 B.C.E.). The body was now regularly placed on its back, rather than its side as had been done for thousands of years. Coffin texts and wooden

83. *Relief of a Fowler.* From Thebes, Egypt. New Kingdom, first half of Dynasty 18, circa 1539–1425 B.C.E. Limestone, 20 ½ x 16 ⁹⁄₁₆ x 1 in. (52 x 42 x 2.5 cm). Gift of Christos G. Bastis in honor of Bernard V. Bothmer, 80.38

Reliefs depicting the deceased performing acts from daily life, as in this bird-hunting scene, lined the tomb chapels of the elite in the New Kingdom. Here the deceased holds a bird decoy in his hand.

models disappeared from new tombs of the period, while heart scarabs and figurines shaped like mummies were now often included in burials, as they would be for the remainder of Egyptian history. Coffin decoration was simplified, eliminating texts and using the palace-facade motif to decorate the exterior. These changes might be associated with political changes that occurred in the reign of Senwosret III (figure 80). Clearly, in this period of more strongly centralized government, religious customs were revised to help explain governmental reforms. Yet the details of how politics and religion interacted in this case continue to elude modern observers.

In the Thirteenth Dynasty, decoration changed again. Different motifs were found in the north and in the south, a reflection of decentralized governmental power at that time.

Elite burials at court in the north included a body in an anthropoid coffin or with a mummy mask, and which was placed, in turn, in a rectangular wooden coffin. The whole was put into a third coffin, of wood or stone. Scepters or staffs of office were buried in the innermost coffin, sometimes with elaborate jewelry. A box now held the four canopic jars. Another box held seven vessels for the seven sacred oils used during the funeral ceremony. An additional box held royal insignia and weapons. Pottery in the tomb in great quantities probably represented food offerings. These burials are quite rare but show the practice among the elite of including many objects emphasizing a person's high status in this life.

Those of lower rank now included in their tombs magical items that were also used in life. Faience statuettes of hippopotami (figure 32), stylized figurines of women (figures 81, 82), and wands made of ivory began to be included in tombs in this period. There were fewer inscriptions on coffins but papyrus was sometimes placed inside them, inscribed not only with religious texts but also, on occasion, with works of literature.

There was also a marked increase in the number of multiple burials in one tomb, a rare occurrence in earlier periods. The reuse of one tomb by a family over the generations seems to have occurred when wealth was more equitably spread. The phenomenon is also found in the Nineteenth Dynasty.

The poorest people were buried in shallow pits with pots, little different from their distant ancestors. Innovation seems to have been a privilege of the rich.

Second Intermediate Period: Burials of Non-Egyptians. Known graves from the Second Intermediate Period reveal the presence of non-Egyptians buried in the country. In the north, graves associated with the Hyksos, a western

84

Semitic people ruling the north from the northeast delta, include small
mud-brick structures containing the body, pottery vessels, a dagger in men's
graves, and often a nearby donkey burial. Simple pan-shaped graves in
various parts of the country are thought to belong to Nubian soldiers. Such
graves reflect very ancient customs and feature shallow, round pits, bodies
contracted, and minimal food offerings in pots. The occasional inclusion of
identifiable Egyptian materials from the Second Intermediate Period
provides the only marks distinguishing these burials from those of the
Predynastic and even earlier periods.

Some Egyptian graves are known from the end of the Second
Intermediate Period. The burial of an official named Hornakht contained
luxury goods such as a wooden headrest, an Old Kingdom calcite vessel,
and a wooden canopic box. It is impossible to generalize about the tombs
of this period from such limited evidence.

New Kingdom: From Objects of Daily Life to Objects for the Afterlife.

The majority of elite tombs in the New Kingdom were rock-cut chambers.
Kings were buried in multiroomed, rock-cut tombs in the Valley of the
Kings and no longer in pyramids. Priests conducted funerary rituals for
them in stone temples built on the west bank of the Nile opposite Thebes
(modern-day Luxor). In the early Eighteenth Dynasty, high officials built
mud-brick, decorated chapels located over a rock-cut burial shaft. Later,
officials replaced these mud-brick structures with rock-cut, decorated
chapels in the mountain bordering the floodplain of the west bank of the
Nile opposite Thebes; figure 83 shows what some of these chapel decorations
looked like. The undecorated burial chambers for these tombs were cut into
the rock below the decorated chapels. People of lower rank continued to
construct mud-brick chapels, which today are so poorly preserved that little
can be said about them.

From current evidence, the Eighteenth Dynasty appears to be the last
period in which the Egyptians regularly included multiple objects from their
daily lives in their tombs; beginning in the Nineteenth Dynasty, tombs
contained fewer items from daily life and included objects made specially for
the next world. Thus the change from the Eighteenth to the Nineteenth
Dynasties formed a dividing line in burial traditions: the Eighteenth Dynasty
more closely resembled the immediate past in its customs; the Nineteenth
Dynasty, in contrast, anticipated the customs of the Late Period.

People of the elite ranks in the Eighteenth Dynasty placed furniture as
well as clothing and other items in their tombs, objects they undoubtedly

84. *Single-Strand Necklace with Taweret Amulets.* From Thebes, Egypt. New Kingdom, probably late Dynasty 18, circa 1332–1292 B.C.E. Faience, 7 15/16 in. (20.2 cm) long. Gift of Mrs. Lawrence Coolidge and Mrs. Robert Woods Bliss, and the Charles Edwin Wilbour Fund, 48.66.42

Jewelry from this world could be worn in the netherworld. This necklace made up of figures of Taweret—protector of pregnant women—would protect the deceased while being reborn into the next world.

85. *Kohl Tube in the Form of a Fish.* Provenance not known. New Kingdom, probably Dynasty 18, circa 1539–1292 B.C.E. Alabaster, 1 ⅝ x ¾ x 4 ⅜ in. (4.2 x 1.9 x 11.1 cm). Museum Collection Fund, 11.668

Kohl was used in ordinary life as eyeliner. The fish was considered a fertility symbol. This container provided storage for kohl in this life and the next, but also symbolized fertility and rebirth in the tomb.

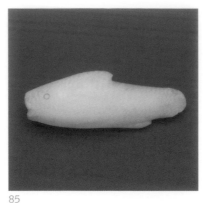

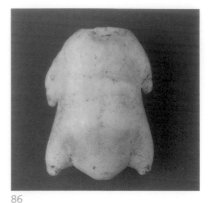

85

86

86. *Hollow Figure of a Trussed Duck.* Provenance not known. New Kingdom, Dynasty 18, circa 1539–1292 B.C.E. Alabaster, 3 x 2 ½ x 4 ⅝ in. (7.6 x 6.4 x 11.7 cm). Museum Collection Fund, 11.667

This storage container doubled as a food offering. Trussed ducks were regularly depicted on offering tables among the delicacies provided for eating in the next world.

87. *Rectangular Toilet Spoon with Handle.* Provenance not known. New Kingdom, Dynasty 18, circa 1539–1292 B.C.E. Wood, 1 ³⁄₁₆ x 1 ⁹⁄₁₆ x 5 ⁵⁄₁₆ in. (3 x 4 x 13.5 cm). Charles Edwin Wilbour Fund, 37.618E

Spoonlike objects such as this were associated with cosmetics and were for use in this world and the next.

87

88

88. *Gaming Board Inscribed for Amenhotep III with Separate Sliding Drawer and a Set of Thirteen Gaming Pieces.* From Egypt. New Kingdom, Dynasty 18, reign of Amenhotep III, circa 1390–1353 B.C.E. Faience, glazed; gaming board: 2 ³/₁₆ x 3 ¹/₁₆ x 8 ¼ in. (5.5 x 7.7 x 21 cm); eight reel-shaped gaming pieces, each ½ in. (1.3 cm) high x ¹³/₁₆ in. (2 cm) diameter; five cone-shaped gaming pieces, each 1 in. (2.6 cm) high x ¹¹/₁₆ in. (1.7 cm) diameter. Charles Edwin Wilbour Fund, 49.56a–b (board), 49.57.1–.13 (pieces)

Board games were played during life and in the netherworld.

89. *Amulet in the Form of a Tyt.* From Egypt. Possibly New Kingdom, circa 1539–1075 B.C.E. Jasper, 2 ³/₈ x 1 x ³/₁₆ in. (6 x 2.5 x 0.5 cm). Charles Edwin Wilbour Fund, 37.1271E

Amulets for the tomb were made to be wrapped inside the mummy. A tyt was the knot in Isis' belt. The amulet was always made of jasper. After placing it over the throat of the mummy, the priest recited Spell 156 from The Book of the Dead, *calling for the magical protection of the limbs.*

used during life on earth. Among the furniture can be found beds, headrests (figure 60), chairs, stools, and wooden storage chests. Other items from this life put into tombs were jewelry (figure 84), cosmetic containers (figure 85) and spoons for preparing cosmetics (figure 87), mirrors (figure 74), weapons, board games (figure 88), and musical instruments. Sandals were included among the clothing; garments could be made of wool, linen, or leather.

Among the Eighteenth Dynasty objects included in tombs that were not used in this life were anthropoid coffins (figure 114) and mummy masks, papyrus *Books of the Dead* (figure 116), heart scarabs (now in wider use than previously; figures 19, 20), amulets (figure 89), and *shabties* (figures 90, 91).

All of the objects described and illustrated so far belonged to an elite rank of people, and few of them were included in the burials of the poor. Farmers, for example, may or may not have had a coffin and mummy mask and might have had weapons or cosmetic containers in graves belonging, respectively, to males and females. Such graves, however, entirely lacked objects bearing writing: *Books of the Dead,* heart scarabs, amulets, and *shabties.* These objects were reserved for the elite.

Shabties illustrate how such objects originated among the elite and only later became available to other ranks of society. All the preserved *shabties* of the Eighteenth Dynasty exhibit a high level of craftsmanship and are often made from precious materials. (This formulation excludes the possibility

89

90. *Shabty of the Scribe Amunemhat.* From Thebes, Egypt. New Kingdom, Dynasty 18, reign of Thutmose IV to reign of Akhenaten, circa 1400–1336 B.C.E. Wood, 8 ⁷⁄₁₆ x 2 ½ x 1 ¾ in. (21.5 x 6.3 x 4.4 cm). Charles Edwin Wilbour Fund, 50.129

This fine wood shabty *with its matching box (see figure 91) belonged to a high-level scribe and was made for the tomb. Forty* shabties *were an ideal number to own in the Ramesside Period. They could then include enough workers for each of the thirty days of the month plus overseers and foremen.*

90

that the Egyptians considered wax figures found in some tombs *shabties.*) In the New Kingdom, *shabties* were carved from limestone and painted (figure 7), as if they were intended to rival in quality tomb sculptures of the deceased. They could also be made of imported wood (figure 90), a material known to be expensive because of its rarity. *Shabties* were stored in skillfully made wooden boxes (figure 91), also a rare commodity. In the Late Period, several hundred years afterward, *shabties* would become widely available in faience for both the elite and people of lesser means. For the royal family and very high courtiers, stone *shabties* continued to be made, but a much wider

91

91. *Shabty Box of Amunemhat.* From Thebes, Egypt. New Kingdom, Dynasty 18, reign of Thutmose IV to reign of Akhenaten, circa 1400–1336 B.C.E. Wood, 12 ½ x 4 ⅛ x 5 in. (31.7 x 10.5 x 12.7 cm). Charles Edwin Wilbour Fund, 50.130a–b

Very fine shabties (see figure 90) were stored in specially made boxes like this one.

group of people would have access to *shabties* of lesser quality and less precise materials in later periods.

Beginning in the reign of Amenhotep III (1390–1353 B.C.E.), Egyptian coffin makers developed several innovations. The elite made use of stone anthropoid sarcophagi in their tombs for the first time. Also, people of lesser means began to use anthropoid coffins made of local wood with yellow-painted backgrounds, perhaps imitating gold (see figures 34, 114); it is also possible that the increasing importance of the sun god in funerary religion during this time is reflected in the use of the sun's color as a coffin background.

92. *Funerary Vessel of the Wab-priest of Amon, Nefer-her, Painted to Imitate Stone.* From Thebes, Egypt. New Kingdom, mid-Dynasty 18 to early Dynasty 19, circa 1479–1279 B.C.E. Pottery, painted, 8 ¼ in. (21 cm) high x 4 ⁷⁄₁₆ in. (11.2 cm) diameter. Charles Edwin Wilbour Fund, 37.343E

Made for the tomb, this pottery vessel was painted to imitate granite, a much more expensive material.

92

93. *Pyramidion of a Woman* (see also figure 9 for an alternate view). From Egypt. New Kingdom to Third Intermediate Period, Dynasty 20 to Dynasty 22, circa 1185–718 B.C.E. Limestone, 8 ⁹⁄₁₆ x 8 ¹⁄₁₆ x 5 ⅛ in. (21.8 x 20.5 x 13 cm). Charles Edwin Wilbour Fund, 05.336

Small pyramids inscribed with the deceased worshipping Osiris are found in Ramesside tombs and slightly later.

No elite tombs survive unplundered from the Ramesside period. But the family tomb of an artist named Sennedjem did survive intact, revealing middle-class funerary traditions. It is thus still possible to comment on tomb decorations and contents for different ranks of people.

In the Ramesside Period, artists decorated tombs belonging to the elite with more scenes of religious events, rather than the everyday scenes that had been popular since the Old Kingdom. The funeral itself (figure 45), the funerary meal with multiple relatives, the worshipping of the gods (figures 9, 93), and even figures in the underworld (figure 26) were subjects in elite

94. *Large Outer Sarcophagus of the Royal Prince, Count of Thebes, Pa-seba-khai-en-ipet.* From Thebes, near Deir el-Bahri, Egypt. Third Intermediate Period, Dynasty 21, circa 1075–945 B.C.E. Wood, gessoed and painted, 37 x 30 ¼ x 83 ⅜ in. (94 x 76.8 x 211.8 cm). Charles Edwin Wilbour Fund, 08.480.1a–b

For unknown reasons, elaborately painted coffins of this period seem to substitute for painted tomb walls.

95. Side view of *Large Outer Sarcophagus of the Royal Prince, Count of Thebes, Pa-seba-khai-en-ipet*

96. Detail of *Large Outer Sarcophagus of the Royal Prince, Count of Thebes, Pa-seba-khai-en-ipet* (see also figure 14)

94

95

96

97. *Shabty of Nesi-ta-nebet-Isheru, Daughter of Pinedjem II.* From Deir el-Bahri, Egypt. Third Intermediate Period, Dynasty 21, circa 1075–945 B.C.E. Faience, glazed, 5 ¹³⁄₁₆ x 2 ¼ x 1 ½ in. (14.7 x 5.7 x 3.8 cm). Gift of Evangeline Wilbour Blashfield, Theodora Wilbour, and Victor Wilbour honoring the wishes of their mother, Charlotte Beebe Wilbour, as a memorial to their father, Charles Edwin Wilbour, 16.183

The inscription on this shabty *commands it to labor in the place of the princess named on it in the event that she is called to work in the netherworld. Shabties could be made of stone or wood, but faience shabties like this one were the most commonly made. By this period, even a princess had faience shabties.*

98. *Shabty of Queen Henuttawy.* From Deir el-Bahri, Egypt. Third Intermediate Period, Dynasty 21, circa 1075–945 B.C.E. Faience, glazed, 4 ⅝ x 1 ¾ x 1 in. (11.7 x 4.5 x 2.6 cm). Gift of Evangeline Wilbour Blashfield, Theodora Wilbour, and Victor Wilbour honoring the wishes of their mother, Charlotte Beebe Wilbour, as a memorial to their father, Charles Edwin Wilbour, 16.188

Members of the royal family used faience *shabties by the Third Intermediate Period.*

99. *Grave Stela of Nehemes-Ra-tawy.* From Thebes, Egypt. Late Period, Dynasty 25 to Dynasty 26, circa 760–656 B.C.E. Limestone, paint, 10 ⅜ x 8 ⅜ x 2 ½ in. (26.4 x 21.3 x 6.4 cm). Charles Edwin Wilbour Fund, 37.588E

A grave stela (an upright stone with an inscription) personalized a shaft tomb, which was essentially a simple hole in the ground, by revealing the name of the deceased.

97

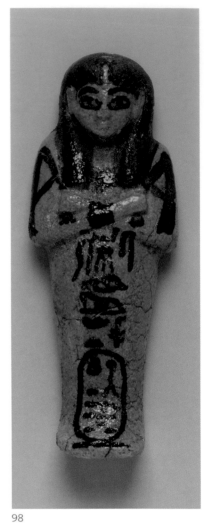

98

tomb decoration. This change remains unexplained except for the fact that royal tombs also exhibit this new emphasis.

Stone sarcophagi were popular among the elite as a resting place for wooden coffins. Among more middle-class officials, anthropoid wooden outer and inner coffins were sometimes used. Within the inner coffin, many people had mummy boards (a board shaped into a life-size figure of the deceased placed directly on the mummy) that sometimes depicted the person in everyday dress. In one case, a woman named Weretwahset combined the lid of her (inner?) coffin with mummy board decoration by portraying herself in a white linen dress on the lid rather than on a mummy board (figure 124); this was perhaps a cost-cutting measure. Poorer people, who could not afford wood, made coffins from painted terracotta. The quality of these coffins varied greatly, but some examples made in molds are excellent imitations of elite products (figure 37).

99

100. *Shabty of the Priest Nes-iswt.* From Campbell's Tomb, Giza, Egypt. Late Period, Dynasty 26, 664–525 B.C.E. Faience, 5 ¾ x 1 ¾ x 1 ¼ in. (14.6 x 4.4 x 3.2 cm). Charles Edwin Wilbour Fund, 37.217E

Faience shabties were used by all classes in the Late Period.

101. *Djed-Column Amulet.* From Egypt. Late Period, Dynasty 26, 664–525 B.C.E. Faience, glazed, 3 ⅞ x ¾ x ¼ in. (9.8 x 1.9 x 0.7 cm). Charles Edwin Wilbour Fund, 08.480.128

Priests placed this amulet on the throat of the mummy and said Spell 155 of The Book of the Dead, *which protected the backbone. The djed-column, symbol of the god Osiris, perhaps represented the human spine.*

100

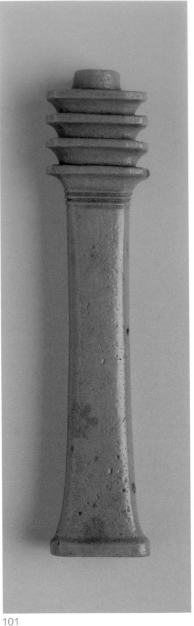

101

The majority of objects found in Ramesside period tombs were made for the afterlife. Aside from some jewelry, which could have been used also during life, objects in Ramesside tombs were manufactured for the next world. *Shabties* for the elite, *Books of the Dead* (figure 116), and even vessels (figure 92) all seem to have been made for the tomb.

Third Intermediate Period: Transitions in Funerary Customs. Though the political structure of the New Kingdom collapsed at the end of the Twentieth Dynasty, the majority of burials in the Twenty-first Dynasty directly reflect

102

102. *Wadjet-Eye Amulet.* From Egypt. Late Period, 664–332 B.C.E. Faience, 2 ⅛ x 1 ¾ x ⅜ in. (5.4 x 4.4 x 0.9 cm). Charles Edwin Wilbour Fund, 08.480.129

Wadjet-eye amulets were believed to have great protective powers. They healed the incision made by the embalmers. The wadjet *was a human eye with the markings of a falcon.*

103. *Eye Amulet.* From Saqqara, Egypt. Dynasties 27–30 , 525–343 B.C.E. Gold, ⁹⁄₁₆ x ³⁄₁₆ x ¹¹⁄₁₆ in. (1.5 x 0.5 x 1.7 cm). Charles Edwin Wilbour Fund, 37.795E

103

developments from the earlier period. At the beginning of this time, reliefs resembled those from the Ramesside period (figures 9, 93). Only at the very end of the Second Intermediate Period, during the Twenty-fifth Dynasty, did the new funerary practices of the Late Period begin to be seen.

Little is known of tombs of this period. Indeed, the very lack of decoration in tombs seems to have led to much more elaborate decoration of coffins: the multiple scenes found on Ramesside tomb walls of gods of the next world and worship of those gods were now transferred to the coffin itself (figure 94). The remaining grave goods of the period show fairly

cheaply made *shabties,* even when the owner was a queen or a princess (figures 97, 98).

Late Period: Monumentality and a Return to Older Traditions.
Burials in the Late Period could make use of large-scale, templelike tombs built for the non-royal elite for the first time. But the majority of tombs in this period were in shafts sunk into the desert floor. In addition to fine statuary and reliefs reflecting the style of the Old Kingdom, the majority of grave goods were specially made for the tomb. Coffins continued to bear religious texts and scenes. Some shafts were personalized by the use of a stela with the deceased's prayers and name on it (figure 99). *Shabties* in faience for all classes are known (figure 100). Canopic jars, though often non-functional, continued to be included. Staves and scepters representing the deceased's office in life were often present as well. A figure of either the god Osiris (figure 28) or of the composite deity Ptah-Soker-Osiris could be found, along with heart scarabs (figures 19, 20), both gold and faience examples of *djed*-columns (figure 101), Eye of Horus amulets (figures 102, 103), figures of gods, and images of the deceased's *ba* (figure 23). Tools for the tomb ritual called the "opening of the mouth" as well as "magical bricks" at the four compass points could also be included.

Ptolemaic Period: Hellenistic Influences.
Following Egypt's conquest by Alexander the Great, the country was ruled by the descendants of Ptolemy, one of his generals. This Macedonian Greek family fostered a culture that promoted both Hellenistic and ancient Egyptian ways of life: while many Greek-speaking people living in Alexandria followed the customs of mainland Greece, others adopted Egyptian customs. Egyptians continued to follow their own already ancient traditions.

Very few Ptolemaic tombs are known. Fine temple statuary of the period suggests the possibility of tomb sculpture (page 22) and offering tables (figure 104). Egyptian elite burials still made use of stone sarcophagi (figures 36, 120). *Books of the Dead* and amulets (figure 105) were also still popular. But by the end of the period, *shabties* seem to have disappeared.

Roman Period: Combining Roman and Egyptian Elements.
The Romans conquered Egypt in 30 B.C.E., ending the rule of the last and most famous member of the Ptolemy family, Cleopatra VII. During Roman rule an elite hybrid burial style developed incorporating both Egyptian and Roman elements.

104. *Offering Table for a Buchis Bull.* Excavated at the Bucheum (Bull Cemetery), Armant, Egypt. End of Ptolemaic Period to Roman Period, 200 B.C.E.–300 C.E. Sandstone, 4 5/8 x 13 11/16 x 17 1/4 in. (11.8 x 34.7 x 43.8 cm). Gift of the Egypt Exploration Society, 32.2088

Little is known of Ptolemaic tombs for humans. This offering table was made for the Buchis Bull, an animal sacred to the god Montu and which was buried much like a human upon its death. The offering table in the tomb of the bull in this period suggests that humans had similar offering tables at this time.

105. *Figure of Nefertum.* From Egypt. Ptolemaic Period, 305–30 B.C.E. Faience, 3 ⁷⁄₁₆ x 1 ¼ x ⁹⁄₁₆ in. (8.8 x 3.2 x 1.4 cm). Charles Edwin Wilbour Fund, 71.142

Nefertum, a god born of the lotus flower, is represented on tomb amulets from the Third Intermediate Period to the Ptolemaic Period.

105

Some people of the period were mummified and wrapped in linen bandages. The front of the mummy was often painted with a selection of traditional Egyptian symbols (figure 18). Mummy masks in either traditional Egyptian style (figure 106) or in Roman style (figure 123) could be added to the mummies. Another possibility was a Roman-style mummy portrait (figure 16), executed in encaustic (pigment suspended in wax) on a wooden panel. Sometimes the feet of the mummy were covered (figure 107). An alternative to these coverings was a complete shroud with Egyptian motifs but a portrait in the Roman style (figure 41). Tombs of the elite could also include fine jewelry (figure 108). Many surviving examples of mummy tags (figure 110) suggest a need to identify the mummy either for workers or during transportation to the cemetery.

106. *Mummy Mask of a Man.* From Egypt. Roman Period, early 1st century C.E. Stucco, gilded and painted, 20 ¼ x 13 x 7 ⅞ in. (51.5 x 33 x 20 cm). Charles Edwin Wilbour Fund, 72.57

Roman mummy masks could include traditional Egyptian motifs. Among those here are the winged sun disk on the head, two images of Osiris on the chest, two wadjet eyes, and two images of the goddesses of mourning—Isis and Nephthys. The mummy mask protected the mummy's head and face.

106

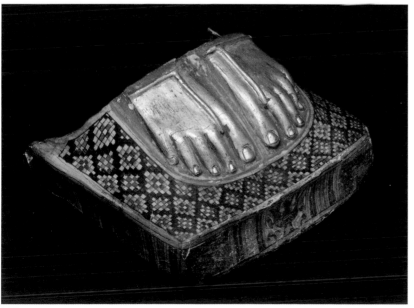

107. *Footcase of a Mummy with Images of Defeated Enemies under the Feet.* From Egypt. Roman Period, circa 1st century C.E. Plaster, painted and gilded, 9 ¹³⁄₁₆ x 10 ³⁄₁₆ x 5 ½ in. (25 x 25.8 x 13.9 cm). Charles Edwin Wilbour Fund, 73.89

The elite covered much of the mummy with gold.

107

108. *Necklace.* From Egypt. Probably Roman Period, 1st–2nd century C.E. Gold, beryl; necklace: 13 9/16 in. (34.4 cm) long; Bes figure: 1 x 7/16 in. (2.6 x 1.1 cm). Gift of Evangeline Wilbour Blashfield, Theodora Wilbour, and Victor Wilbour honoring the wishes of their mother, Charlotte Beebe Wilbour, as a memorial to their father, Charles Edwin Wilbour, 16.149

Beryl beads like these were commonly found in jewelry during the Roman Empire, but the beryl image of Bes included (figure 109) in this necklace is quite rare.

109. Detail of *Necklace*

109

108

Even less is known of non-elite burials in the Roman period. One example of a terracotta sarcophagus is extremely crude (figure 122).

•

Continuity and change, always a theme of the more than 3,500 years of Egyptian history, are clearly present in a review of Egyptian funerary customs such as this. Ideas and customs seem to persist for very long periods, with even the new ideas living long enough to become old. Yet it is also clear that one thing never changed: the elite could always command the best materials and the best craftsmanship, while people living at other levels of society did their best to obtain what they could to ensure their own eternity.

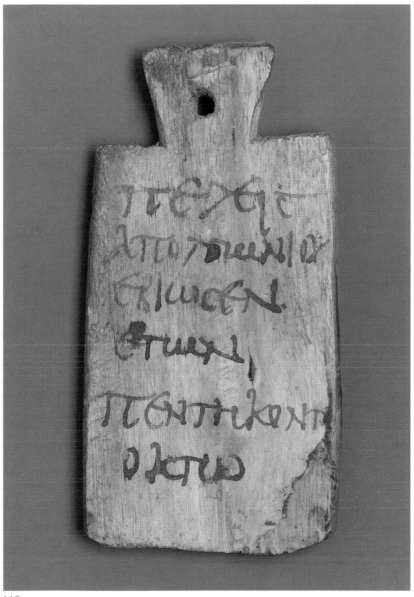

110

110. *Mummy Tag with Greek Inscription.* Possibly collected at Dongola, Sudan. Probably Roman Period, 150–300 C.E. Wood, 4 ½ x 2 ⁵⁄₁₆ x ⅜ in. (11.4 x 5.8 x 1 cm). Charles Edwin Wilbour Fund, 37.1396E

Mummy tags identify the deceased by name. In the Roman Period, the Egyptians stopped using coffins. Though the deceased's name might also be inscribed on the shroud, a mummy tag provided additional insurance that the name would be associated with the mummy.

How Much Did a Coffin Cost?

The Social and Economic Aspects of Funerary Arts in Ancient Egypt

Kathlyn M. Cooney

In ancient Egypt, *things* were essential for the dead. When preparing the dead for burial, the Egyptians made a direct connection between magical-religious power and tangible, material objects. They created innumerable things—tombs, coffins, amulets, figurines, illuminated guidance books—and even preserved the material substance of human bodies through mummification, all for the protection and continued existence of the deceased in the netherworld. Thus, in an early text meant to instruct the younger generation we read the following advice about the material preparations required to live forever:

> Make good your dwelling in the graveyard. Make worthy your station in the West. Given that death humbles us, given that life exalts us, the house of death is for life.[1]

During mummification rites, opening-of-the-mouth ceremonies, and other protective and transformative rituals, funerary objects received value

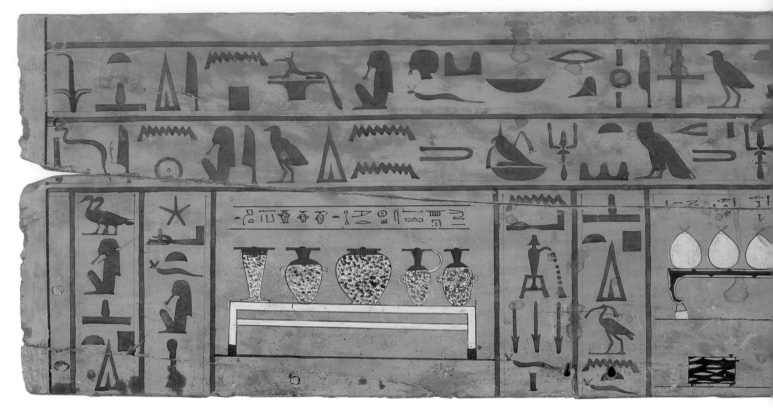

111

111. *Panel from the Coffin of a Woman.* From Asyut, Egypt. Middle Kingdom, late Dynasty 11 to early Dynasty 12, circa 2008–1875 B.C.E. Wood, pigment, 17 ½ x 71 ½ x 1 ¼ in. (44.5 x 181.6 x 3.2 cm). Charles Edwin Wilbour Fund, 1995.112

Coffins painted with the necessities for the tomb—such as mirrors, sandals, or food—made it possible to omit such paintings from the tomb walls. These paintings provided extra protection for the deceased.

112. Detail of *Panel from the Coffin of a Woman*

Embalming materials needed to make the body a mummy were stored on a bed, as depicted here on a coffin or in many scenes from tombs. These representations were believed to ensure provision of all that was needed to make a perfect burial.

as religiously charged pieces, surrounding the dead body with active apotropaic spells and images. In the New Kingdom *Book of the Dead,* prosperity and the ability to act in the next world are often linked to the ownership of funerary objects. For instance, an explanation of *The Book of the Dead,* Chapter 72, probably written by a funerary priest, tells us that the religiously activated coffin and the spells written on it allow provisions and transformative powers for the deceased:

> As for him who knows this book on earth or it is put in writing on the coffin, it is my word that he shall go out into the day in any shape that he desires and shall go into his place without being turned back, and there shall be given to him bread and beer and portion of meat from upon the altar of Osiris.[2]

This funerary text tells us that a material object, in this case the coffin, performed multiple functions after the interment of the deceased: it was transformative, allowing the deceased to assume "any shape that he desires"; it was protective, keeping him from "being turned back"—and it granted the dead economic powers as well, ensuring food and drink in the realm of the afterlife. It is both the coffin itself and the writing on the coffin that grant the deceased these powers. We can see this latter concept expressed quite

clearly on the Middle Kingdom coffin panel of a woman (figure 111) on which are painted a pair of sandals, a fan, oils, stone vessels, and an offering text—all meant magically to provide the woman dwelling inside with everything that she might need in the afterlife. This object could provide the dead not only with sustenance but also with luxury items, so that she could be comfortable in the next life, in accordance with her social and economic status as one who could afford such funerary material. For this reason, Egyptians attempted to prepare for death during their lifetimes. This intense attention to impending death may seem morbid to us, but from their point of view, it was simply a sensible economic and social investment.

The ancient Egyptians also found it useful to buy smaller objects to help the dead in the afterlife, including amulets and figurines. Many *Book of the Dead* spells include instructions in which a specific amulet is required to make a spell efficacious. For example, Chapter 89 includes a spell allowing the *ba* (soul) movement: the soul can ascend to the Sacred Boat of the sun god, and it can also rejoin the corpse in the earthly realm of the necropolis at the end of every day at sundown. *The Book of the Dead* text indicates that the soul seems to require a material object for this spell to be effective:

> The Sacred Boat will be joyful and the Great God will proceed in peace when you allow this soul of mine to ascend vindicated to the gods.... May it [the soul] see my corpse, may it rest on my mummy, which will never be destroyed or perish. To be spoken over a human-headed bird of gold inlaid with semiprecious stones and laid on the breast of the deceased.[3]

This *Book of the Dead* text tells us exactly what material the amulet should be made of. The more precious the amulet, presumably the more powerful: gold was considered the flesh of the gods, and thus an amulet representing the deceased as a winged golden soul (figure 113) would confer upon the corpse the powers of transformation and mobility.

Funerary objects were thought to provide the deceased with magical and superhuman powers in the realm of the tomb and the netherworld—powers that were, so to speak, *embodied* in material objects like coffins and amulets. But we often forget that these objects were also commodities; they had to be commissioned and bought for a particular price. Drawing attention to the fact that ancient individuals had to *pay* for their funerary objects brings new social and economic dynamics into the ongoing Egyptological discussion of funerary religion and rituals. For individuals of differing rank, access to funerary religion and magic was never equal, because there was not universal access to the commodity objects used in ritual activity. Intense and systematic material preparation for the afterlife mirrors a deep psychological preparation for one's inevitable death; but at the same time it also reveals social and economic agendas, showing how the family of the deceased used this opportunity to display its wealth and status before an audience, both in the context of funerary preparation and in the eventual burial rites.

Simply put, traditional elite funerary practice in ancient Egypt was expensive and exclusionary. But rarely do we consider the social and economic costs of these activities to Egyptian individuals and communities, perhaps because our fascination with belief systems as practiced by the elite has suppressed discussion of more worldly and practical aspects. Yet to reach a fuller understanding of how one prepared to live forever, we must not forgo examination of how the ancient Egyptians chose their funerary objects, how much these objects cost, how they were paid for, and what ultimately were the repercussions of the high-priced burial goods market. These are the themes to be pursued in the following pages.

113. *Amulet Representing the Soul as a Human-Head Falcon.* From Saqqara, Egypt. Late Period, 664–332 B.C.E. Gold, ⅞ x 1 ⅝ x ¼ in. (2.2 x 4.2 x 0.6 cm). Charles Edwin Wilbour Fund, 37.805E

Gold amulets were the most powerful, since gold was the flesh of the gods.

Purchasing a Coffin

Our best textual information about the construction and exchange of funerary goods comes from western Thebes, in particular the craftsmen's village of Deir el-Medina, where we find a treasure trove of texts involving the production and value of funerary arts.[4] Egyptologists are often drawn to this New Kingdom village to answer social and economic questions about the ancient Egyptian world because the craftsmen who lived here have left us a rich collection of ostraca (texts written on potsherds or limestone flakes) and papyri dealing with everyday activities: legal documents, letters, receipts, workshop records, official reports, and so on.[5] This west Theban village housed the artisans and workmen who built and decorated the New Kingdom royal tombs in the Valley of the Kings and Valley of the Queens. As royal artisans, such men received a generous monthly wage from the state and displayed a much higher rate of literacy than the majority of the population. They produced thousands of written records and letters concerning their social, economic, legal, and religious activities. Most of the surviving records come from the Ramesside Period, that is, the Nineteenth and Twentieth Dynasties of the New Kingdom, between 1295 and 1069 B.C.E., extending from the reign of Ramesses I to that of Ramesses XI.

114

Because Deir el-Medina was a likely place for many wealthy Egyptians to have purchased their coffins, it provides the best evidence for funerary arts creation and commercial exchange in the New Kingdom.[6]

The most vital piece of equipment for the corpse—the coffin—had to be purchased and paid for. The late Eighteenth Dynasty coffin of the Deir el-Medina craftsman Teti (figure 114) shows us the color and style of many wooden coffins produced later in the Ramesside Period: red, black, white, blue, and green figural decoration was covered with a translucent varnish that turned the white background color a light yellow. Such coffins were constructed from costly materials like wood, pigments, and varnish, and these materials had prices, many of which are preserved in Ramesside commercial texts from Deir el-Medina and associated west Theban worksites. The price of a coffin was determined by a number of variables, some clearly expressed in the textual material, some not, including the cost of materials like wood and paint, the cost of the craftsman's time, the reputation and skill level of the maker, the length and quality of the religious texts to be included, the types of scenes painted on the coffin, and the quality level of the craftsmanship.

The records of coffin prices from Deir el-Medina provide an understanding of the pieces' exchange value. The Deir el-Medina corpus preserves 168 prices for different coffin types, which represent a huge range in the perceived value of funerary objects. Most prices for coffins were recorded in copper *deben*—that is, 91 grams, equivalent to the cost of about 10 loaves of bread. In New Kingdom Egypt, 5 *deben* could buy you a goat or a pair of sandals or a woven linen shirt.[7] In general, 25 *deben* could buy you a decent-quality anthropoid (or person-shaped) coffin made of wood and decorated with figural designs. Table 1 (page 118) shows the average price, the median (or most common) price, and the high and low prices for different types of coffins, including the standard anthropoid coffin (*wet* in Egyptian), the outer coffin (*men-ankh / wet a'a* in Egyptian), the inner coffin (*wet sheri*), and the mummy board (*sukhet*), a wooden cover that fit over the mummy inside of the anthropoid coffin. Some of these records are not well preserved and are difficult to read, resulting in some insecure prices. The "secure" prices are therefore averaged separately to check the data. The "average" price in this chart represents the total amount of money divided by the number of prices. The "median" price represents the most common one in a series of prices. The "average without high and low" does not include the most expensive nor the cheapest prices of a particular coffin type.

114. *Anthropoid Coffin of the Servant of the Great Place, Teti* (see also figure 34). From Thebes, Egypt. New Kingdom, mid- to late Dynasty 18, circa 1339–1307 B.C.E. Wood, painted, 33 ¼ x 18 ¹³⁄₁₆ x 81 ½ in. (84.5 x 47.8 x 207 cm). Charles Edwin Wilbour Fund, 37.14E

Coffins painted with red, black, white, blue, and green were varnished, turning the background yellow. Such coffins became typical in the Nineteenth Dynasty. This is a very early example of the type.

Object Category	Average of All Prices	Average of Secure Prices	Median of All Prices	High Price(s)	Low Price(s)	Average without High and Low
wet (mummiform coffin)	31.57	29.67	25	220 (-x?) & 145	4 (?) & 8	24.61
wet decoration	10.5	12.14	10	65	2 & 2.5	9.38
wet construction	22.75	35.66	10.25	80	9 (?)	11.87
wet carving	4	2.5	2	10 (?)	1	3
wet wood	4.4	5	5	5	1 (?)	5
men-ankh / wet a'a (outer coffin)	37.5	40.8	32.5	95	15 (?)	31.6
men-ankh / wet a'a decoration	16.31	16.25	17.5	35	5	15.08
wet sheri (inner coffin) decoration	16.83	21.25	9	60	5	9
sukhet (mummy board)	25.9	25.9	22.5	34	15	26.25
sukhet decoration	5	6.5	5	14	3 (?)	4.64

Table 1. Average prices for coffins (in *deben*) according to Deir el-Medina textual material

An item's price provides only a limited understanding of its value as a funerary object, but it is a useful beginning. For example, in one Ramesside text, Ostracon Deir el-Medina 146,[8] we read:

> List of all the work which I did for the deputy Amennakht: 2 *qeniu* seats making 30 (*deben*), wood: 1 *Hati* bed making 20 *deben*, 1 *wet* coffin making 25 *deben*. The excess thereof: 48 (*deben*). Wood: 1 *tut* statue making 15 *deben*, 1 *kesekesti* box making 3 *deben*. Total 93 copper *deben*.

This workshop record seems to have been written by an unnamed craftsman (probably a carpenter) to record a completed commission ordered by the deputy Amennakht for wooden objects, including a chair, a bed, a coffin, and a statue, for a total of 93 *deben*—a very large sum of copper for a craftsman who earned about 11 *deben* a month.[9]

In another text dating to the reign of Ramesses III (Ostracon Ashmolean Museum HO 183),[10] we learn a great deal of information about the value of expensive pigments when used in funerary arts:

> To inform about all the commissions which the workman Prehotep did for Amenem-di-raneb: 1 *wet* coffin, varnished, its *qenekh* body part (?) being green and its *neshi* body part (?) being yellow

orpiment, making 40 *deben,* precious wood: [...], 1 *sukhet* mummy
board, varnished and decorated, making 25 *deben.*

The price for a finished *wet* coffin in this text is 40 *deben,* about 15 *deben*
higher than the most common (median) price for this funerary object type
(average 31.57 *deben;* median 25 *deben*). The text notes green and yellow
orpiment paint specifically, both expensive pigments, suggesting that these
materials may have been part of the reason for the higher price.

Commercial texts from Deir el-Medina tell us about the material value
of crafted objects, including what type of object is being sold, what
materials it is made of, who made it, and how much it costs. Just like our
modern supermarket receipt, these ancient commercial texts record only
particular sorts of information: the manufacturer (in this case the
craftsmen), the price (here usually in the form of copper *deben*), the
details of the exchange (if specific commodities changed hands to make
payment), and the names of the buyers. The means of production and
exchange are the focus in these texts; the material nature of the
commodities changing hands is carefully recorded in terms of price, type,
and maker. But contextual details about why a particular purchase was
made, how much discussion the purchase required, how a particular
craftsman was chosen by the buyer, or the quality level of craftsmanship are
not mentioned in any of these texts. Non-contextualized information like
names and prices provides only a vague indication of the quality of a
particular piece of funerary art because we are not part of this ancient
commercial system. The name and title of a specific craftsman may have
been a key measure for locals to judge his reputation and the perceived
quality of the commissioned funerary piece, but we, as modern outsiders,
have little insight into the real-world details of order, production, and
exchange. To draw a loose analogy: essentially, we are trying to understand
ancient craft specialization and value from a small collection of torn and
fragmented supermarket receipts supplemented by a few memos left to us
by store managers.

In another Twentieth Dynasty text dating to the reign of Ramesses V
(Ostracon Ashmolean Museum HO 163),[11] we have a simple receipt
recording how a priest paid a carpenter for his coffin:

> List of all the property which the *wab* priest Neferhotep paid to
> the carpenter Meryre being the silver of his *wet* coffin: 3 *khar* sacks
> of emmer wheat, 1 braided *kesekeser* basket (making) 1 *khar,*

115. *Canopic Jar and Lid (Depicting a Hawk).* From Egypt, Late Period, Dynasty 26 (or later), 664–525 B.C.E. or later. Limestone, 10 ¼ in. (26 cm) high x 4 ½ in. (11.4 cm) diameter. Charles Edwin Wilbour Fund, 37.895Ea–b

Documents from Deir el-Medina suggest that canopic jars were part of the equipment needed for an elite burial.

1 smooth *meses* shirt making 5 *deben*, 2 braided *kebes* baskets making 2 *oipe*, 1 *tema* mat (and) 1 *deni* basket.

It is clear from these texts that the ancient Egyptians were not using money per se but were nonetheless thinking in monetary terms. The word meaning *silver* in this text is translated literally here, but it could just as easily have been translated as *money*. This text lists, essentially, the *money* that was paid for the coffin, and it takes the form of a collection of objects. That is to say, the ancient Egyptians were trading commodities for other commodities: coffins were traded for baskets, mats, and even livestock. But each commodity was set equal to an amount of copper *deben* or sacks of grain (*khar*), and we therefore read that a given object is said to be "making X amount of copper," that is, each object is worth this much money. The ancient Egyptians set their commodities equal to amounts of copper or grain, creating prices, allowing them to equalize their commercial exchanges. If we add up the prices for all the commodities paid in exchange for the coffin in the above text, we see that the carpenter Meryre received grain, basketry, and linen in the amount of 20 *deben*, more or less, from the *wab* priest. Comparatively, this is not an expensive coffin, but since the man was paying a carpenter, it is possible that he was paying only for an undecorated and unfinished funerary object.

A number of letters from ancient Thebes also mention funerary craftwork, and they provide some of the most interesting real-world details about craft production. For instance, in Papyrus Deir el-Medina 9, also dating to the Twentieth Dynasty,[12] we see a carpenter writing to a man of higher status, a scribe of the vizier:

> (Chief) carpenter of the Lord of the Two Lands Maa-nakhtuef to the scribe Amenmesu of the vizier. Note that I wish to hear of your condition a thousand times a day (because) you did not come within the year. Look, I am painting the *wet sheri* inner coffin together with the *wat* mummy mask. The incense which you brought has almost run out. Please have someone send incense, pistacia pitch, and wax so that I can varnish (it).

The recipient of the letter is Amenmesu, the scribe of the vizier, and he seems to be supplying materials such as incense, pitch, and wax to the carpenter so that the latter can varnish an inner coffin with translucent yellow pistacia resins. As scribe of the vizier, his contacts in the elite bureaucracy would be far-reaching. If this is the case, this scribe could

have been supplying the so-called chief carpenter at Deir el-Medina as part of an informal workshop for the production of private-sector funerary arts of which he seems to be the main organizer.[13] The carpenter was dependent on the scribe for materials to finish his commission, even though he was not making the coffin as part of his work for the royal workshop in the Valley of the Kings.

Another Nineteenth Dynasty letter (Ostracon Černý 19)[14] tells us how Deir el-Medina artisans purchased craft goods and raw materials from different workshops, even for the burial of their own family members:

> Communication of the draftsman Pay to his son the draftsman Pre-em-heb: Please make plans to find the two hearts of faience about which I told you I would pay their price to their owner, namely anything he will ask as their price. And make plans to search out this fresh incense that I told you about in order to varnish the *wet* coffin of your mother. I gave its price [to] its owner.... Do not be neglectful about all that I have told you, yourself.

In this text, a son is instructed to buy two heart amulets from a workshop specializing in faience, presumably heart scarabs similar to a later example made of steatite and gold (see figures 19, 20). The son is also told by his father to fetch incense resins so that they can apply the translucent yellow varnish to the coffin of his own mother. It is not known whether his mother was dead at this point, but it seems unlikely. Because the ancient Egyptians created their burial equipment far in advance if they could afford funerary arts, it is probable that the man was making a coffin for his wife while she was still alive. In the Egyptian mindset, this behavior was not macabre, but simply practical. Preparing for death required economic investment in crafted material goods.

Other texts from western Thebes are legal in nature and involve court proceedings concerning the purchase of burial goods. In Ostracon Deir el-Medina 225 of the mid-Twentieth Dynasty,[15] we read about a woman named Iy who was brought before the local court:

> Legal contendings of the workman Ameneminet with the lady Iy, the wife of Huy who is deceased. And she said, "I will make a *wet* coffin for my husband, and I will bury him," so she said. And she said to the scribe Amennakht, "I will make a *wet* coffin for Huy and you will take for yourself his hut."

In this text, a woman is taken to court because she did not provide burial equipment for her dead husband, although she presumably received his inheritance, a legal problem if she did not pay for his burial.[16] Although she promises to make (*iri*) the coffin herself, she is in fact promising to pay for it, asking the scribe Amennakht to make it, and in payment she is giving him a hut, or small dwelling (*at* in Egyptian), once belonging to her dead husband.

Purchasing Other Funerary Equipment

Deir el-Medina commercial texts also tell us about the purchase of other burial equipment, such as *shabty* figurines that were thought to labor for the deceased in the afterlife, most of them probably similar to the painted New Kingdom wooden *shabty* of Amunemhat (figure 90). In Ostracon IFAO 764 of the mid-Twentieth Dynasty,[17] we learn that it was possible for an ancient Egyptian during the Ramesside Period to buy a set of forty such *shabty* figurines, presumably one for each day of the thirty-day month with additional foremen and overseers to make sure they did their work:

> The decoration of the chief workman Nekhemut [...]: 40 *shabties* making 1 *deben* (and) making 15 *deben* (for) the *wet* coffin and the *yetit* funerary object [...]

In addition to the forty *shabties* mentioned in this text, this craftsman also decorated an entire set of funerary equipment, including an anthropoid coffin and a funerary object that may have been some form of mummy board (*yetit* in Egyptian).[18] The *shabty* figurines are the least expensive part of this funerary equipment by far, costing only 1 *deben* to paint them, compared to 15 *deben* to paint the larger body containers. The *shabty* figurines are important, but the body containers take precedence; at least this is what the prices tell us.

Another Twentieth Dynasty receipt (Ostracon Liverpool 13626)[19] lists a *shabty* box among a number of other burial items. The painted box meant to contain the *shabty* figurines was probably similar to the Eighteenth Dynasty example of Amunemhat in shape (figure 91) and, at only 2 *deben*, was quite inexpensive compared to the total price of 112 *deben* for all the craftwork listed in this text:

> 1 large *men-ankh* outer coffin making [...] *deben*, wood:
> 1 woman's *men-ankh* outer coffin making [...] *deben*, a *wet sheri*

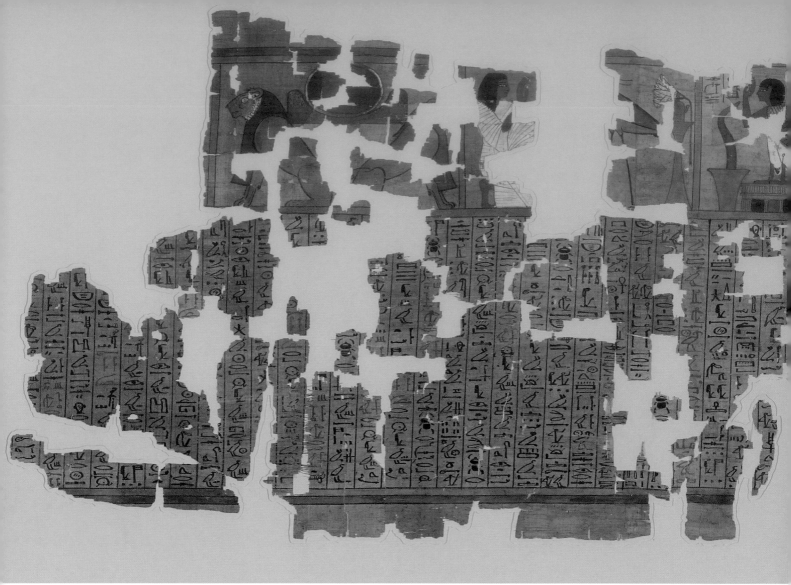

116

inner coffin on which I did *seqer.ef* (?) work on its arms (?) and *mesha* work strengthening i[ts] front of the feet together with its *ama'a* body part (?) [making] 5 (*deben*), wood: 2 *sheger* containers making 3 *deben*, wood: 1 *iter shabty* box making 2 *deben*, 1 braided *kebes* basket making 1 *deben*, 1 *tema* mat and 1 *merekh* sieve making 1 *deben*, 3 sacks of good blue pigment, 1 *wet* coffin, sawn wood prepared (?) for its *gati* canopic chest. Total of all the work which I did for [him]: 112 (*deben*).

In other texts, we learn that Ramesside individuals could buy canopic jars (the funerary containers that held the liver, lungs, intestines, and stomach of the mummified deceased) and the wooden canopic chests that held these jars. The Twentieth Dynasty Ostracon Deir el-Medina 679[20] tells of the sale of canopic jars along with an entire set of funerary equipment, including an inner and outer coffin, indicating that the mummification and the associated viscera containers were part of an elite burial:

What the draftsman Menna sold to the Songstress of Amen Henutwati: 1 painted *wet a'a* outer coffin, 4 canopic jars, and 1 painted *wet sheri* inner coffin.

Unfortunately, no prices are listed in this document, but it does tell us that Theban purchasers came to the village of Deir el-Medina to buy entire sets of coffins as well as containers for mummified internal organs. These canopic jars would have resembled the Late Period example seen in figure 115, at least in form, but they would have been made of wood and painted with bright colors, in accordance with Ramesside west Theban styles.

Another text, Papyrus Berlin P 10485,[21] tells of the sale of canopic jars and a canopic chest to contain them, among a number of other wooden craft items:

This day of noting all that I sold to[.... That] which I gave to him: my *qebeu-en-wet* canopic jars making 5 *deben*, 1 *gaut* canopic chest

116. *The Book of the Dead of Neferrenpet.* From Thebes, Egypt. New Kingdom, Dynasty 19, circa 1295–1185 B.C.E. Painted papyrus, 17 ½ x 48 ½ in. (44.5 x 123.2 cm). Gift of Theodora Wilbour, 35.1448a–d and 35.1464

A painted papyrus such as this became more widely available to a priest and scribe like Neferrenpet during the Nineteenth Dynasty. Previously such information was restricted to the royal circle.

117

117. *Sun on the Horizon.* Detail from *The Book of the Dead of Neferrenpet*

The sun on the horizon, depicted between two mountain peaks, is the hieroglyphic writing for part of Re-Horakhty's name. This god is the form the sun takes when it rises and when it sets.

making 10 *deben*, wood: 1 *khati* bed making 20 *deben*, wood: 1 *qeniu* seat making 20 *deben*, (1) *had* footstool [making] 1 *deben*, 2 smooth *daiu* garments making 20 *deben*, wood: 1 *gaut* chest making [10?] *deben* [...] 1 *masha* object [making 15 (?) *deben*] [...] making 120 *deben*.

All of these objects are said to be crafted of wood. The canopic jars are said to cost 5 *deben*, while the accompanying canopic chest cost 10 *deben*, both lower than the median price for the anthropoid coffin at 25 *deben* (see Table 1). Proportionally, then, the coffin seems to have been the most expensive and the most important funerary investment for the deceased, according to this textual material. Consumers always paid more for their coffin than they did for accessories like *shabties* and canopic jars.

It was also the practice of wealthy Egyptians to purchase *Book of the Dead* papyri, according to the commercial Deir el-Medina texts, and they probably looked very similar to the Nineteenth Dynasty fragmentary example of Neferrenpet (figures 116–118). The economic texts tell us there was a wide range in prices, and presumably aesthetic value. One document dating to the thirty-sixth year of Ramesses II of the Nineteenth Dynasty (Ostracon Ashmolean Museum HO 133)[22] mentions the exchange of two *Books of the Dead,* one illuminated with polychrome scenes and the other undecorated:

What was paid by Neferabet to the draftsman Rahotep in exchange for the *khenu* chapel: 1 fine, thin *ifed* sheet making 3 (?) *seniu,* 1 decorated *Book of the Dead* papyrus making 1 *deben* (of silver)

118

and 3 *heneu* sesame oil.... What is given to him in exchange for the *wet* coffin of the guard Khawy: a papyrus roll of *The Book of the Dead* of Amenmesu making 3 *seniu.*

All of the prices in this Nineteenth Dynasty text are in silver (measured in *deben,* weighing 91 grams, and *seniu,* weighing 7.6 grams)[23] rather than copper, and the price of the illuminated *Book of the Dead* text mentioned in this receipt is 1 silver *deben,* about 60 to 100 copper *deben* (depending on the exchange rate between copper and silver), an extraordinarily high price given that the monthly salary of the Deir el-Medina craftsman was about 11 copper *deben.* The second *Book of the Dead,* said to belong to Amenmesu, is not described as painted, and it is therefore priced at only 3 *seniu,* or about 15 copper *deben.* This text provides us with a good idea of the economic value of a draftsman's skill and time: *The Book of the Dead* illuminated with colorful scenes of afterlife existence is four to six times more expensive than the version with only text. In other words, the cost of the draftsman's effort was much more expensive than either the papyrus material or the scribe's text. Only the very wealthy consumer could afford such an illuminated papyrus; other individuals had to make do with only the magical text.

Buying within One's Price Range

Few individuals in ancient Egypt could afford the ideal set of coffins and funerary equipment—consisting of three nesting coffins, a mummy mask, canopic jars, a canopic chest, and *shabty* figurines. Only the very rich could

118. *Priest in a White Garment.* Detail from *The Book of the Dead of Neferrenpet*

The priest, nearest the stern of the boat, is accompanied by mourners and officials, all in white linen garments.

afford gold; most of the elite made do with wood and some gilding. Even King Tutankhamun benefited from solid-gold construction only in his mask and inner coffin; among his other, gilded-wood pieces, his second coffin may actually have been usurped from another ruler and redecorated for him.[24] Lack of funds and unexpected circumstances necessitated negotiation and adaptation by every ancient Egyptian. Buyers negotiated their desire for religiously charged objects (among them a body transformed through mummification, a coffin, a tomb, canopic jars, and figurines) with their ability to pay for them, resulting in funerary arts spanning a range of prices and quality levels. Some funerary objects were carefully made with high-quality materials; others were produced with cheap materials by artisans who lacked high-level training in the palace workshops, sponsored by the king and temples. Comparing two objects in the exhibition illustrates this contrast. The Brooklyn Museum's coffin of Pa-seba-khai-en-ipet (figure 94) is a high-cost Twenty-first Dynasty coffin painted by a skilled draftsman with detailed scenes using generous amounts of expensive blue and green paints; it is the outermost in a three-piece coffin set of two coffins and a mummy board. The craftsman responsible was probably state-trained, and the buyer was a part of the Egyptian elite. On the other hand, individuals who were not able to afford such expensive objects might purchase something like the exhibition's late Sixth Dynasty funerary statuette of limestone (figure 119), which is very simply carved and painted by an unskilled craftsman with cheap red, black, and white paints.

The situation was the same with mummification. It is well known to forensic scientists that there was a wide range of quality in body preparation in ancient Egypt: some corpses were fully embalmed, such as the Roman Period body of a man named Demetrios (figure 17), in contrast to others that were simply washed and wrapped. The Greek historian Herodotus described the mummification methods of the ancient Egyptians within the context of the marketplace, discussing differing qualities and expenses:

> Mummification is a distinct profession. The embalmers, when a body is brought to them, produce specimen models in wood, painted to resemble nature, and graded in quality; the best and most expensive kind is said to represent a being whose name I shrink from mentioning in this connection; the next best is somewhat inferior and cheaper, while the third sort is cheapest of all. After pointing out these differences in quality, they ask which of the

119

119. *Statuette of a Striding Man.* Provenance not known. Old Kingdom, late Dynasty 6, circa 2288–2170 B.C.E. Limestone, painted, 6 ⅝ x 3 ¹⁄₁₆ x 1 ¾ in. (16.9 x 7.7 x 4.4 cm). Gift of Evangeline Wilbour Blashfield, Theodora Wilbour, and Victor Wilbour honoring the wishes of their mother, Charlotte Beebe Wilbour, as a memorial to their father, Charles Edwin Wilbour, 16.238

Limestone statues such as this one were easier to carve and were often less expensive than statues of harder stone such as granite.

three is required, and the kinsmen of the dead man, having agreed upon a price, go away and leave the embalmers to their work.[25]

Although Herodotus wrote this description of commercial activity a millennium after the New Kingdom, the process of coffin commission and production in Deir el-Medina was probably not very different. Ostensibly, prospective clients made contact with craftsmen, discussed the different funerary objects and quality levels available to them, communicated what they could afford, and, we should assume, after a great deal of haggling, agreed on a price.

120. *Sarcophagus Lid of Pa-di-Djehuti.* From cemetery at el-Tarmakiya, near Hardai (Kynopolis), Egypt. Ptolemaic Period, circa 305–30 B.C.E. Limestone, 80 5/16 x 22 13/16 x 13 3/8 in. (204 x 58 x 34 cm). Charles Edwin Wilbour Fund, 34.1221

The burial of the sarcophagus was the last act of the funeral. A heavy stone example like this one would have been transported on a sledge.

120

121. *Head and Bust of an Official in a Double Wig.* Provenance not known. New Kingdom, Dynasty 18, reign of Amunhotep III, circa 1390–1353 B.C.E. Granodiorite, 4 ½ x 4 ⁹⁄₁₆ x 3 ¾ in. (11.4 x 11.6 x 9.6 cm). Gift of the Ernest Erickson Foundation, Inc., 86.226.28

Granodiorite was a rare stone available only to the elite for statues used in the tomb.

Some families could afford to spend a great deal on funerary equipment; others made do with very little. Some Deir el-Medina texts, such as Ostracon Turin 57368[26] of the mid- to late Twentieth Dynasty, document the purchase of very expensive coffins:

> List of the silver which the scribe of the tomb Hori sold: 1 *wet* coffin of *isy* tamarisk wood making 80 (*deben*), the decoration and that which was varnished making 65 copper *deben*, a *sukhet* mummy board […] making 20 (*deben*). Receiving from him (as payment):[27] 1 ox making 100 *deben*. Receiving from him: another ox making 100 (+x?) *deben*, 1 smooth *dayet* cloak making 20 (*deben*), making 43 *deben*, a smooth *ifet* sheet making 8 (*deben*), the *sukhet* mummy board making 15 (*deben*).

In this text, the cost for a *wet* coffin is 145 *deben*—a very high price. The construction of this *wet* coffin cost 80 *deben*, a substantial investment for a piece without any decoration or finishing; part of the cost must be accounted for in the mention of tamarisk. The fact that tamarisk was noted for a coffin of such expense indicates that this type of wood was economically valued by those commissioning the work and that they specifically asked that this expensive wood be used. Wealthy individuals could afford to demand high-quality materials.

Other texts document the sale of much cheaper anthropoid coffins, often purchased by individuals who could afford only one coffin and maybe also a mummy mask. For example, Ostracon Cairo 25601 of the Twentieth Dynasty[28] reads:

> 1 *wet* coffin making 10 (*deben*), a *wet wa* mummy mask (?) 4 (*deben*),
> 1 *wet* coffin making 8 (*deben*), a *wet wa* mummy mask (?) 3 (*deben*),
> a *wet wa* mummy mask (?) 3 (*deben*). Total copper: 28 *deben*.

In this text, one anthropoid coffin costs only 10 *deben* and another only 8 *deben*, much lower than the median price of 25 *deben* for this same type of coffin (see Table 1), and there is nothing in this text to suggest that only decoration or construction is meant. Many people could pay only low prices for their funerary arts, and they were actually the lucky ones: most ancient Egyptians could afford only to wrap their dead family members in a textile of some sort, like a palm rib mat, and inter them in a communal grave.

We often assume that all Egyptians prepared a coffin of some kind for their body, but the textual and archaeological evidence proves that only very few could afford to do so. High costs for materials and labor prohibited most from participating fully in elite funerary culture. The real-world costs of enacting complex belief systems with purchased funerary equipment meant that all individuals were limited in their preparations for the afterlife by the burial goods they could afford. In death and the afterlife, all were not treated as equals.

Funerary Arts and Social Inequality

Spending by the elite on funerary arts not only protected the soul in the afterlife, but could also serve as a form of political and socio-economic maintenance for the deceased's family, showing publicly who belonged to which status groups and why. Some high elite funerary equipment, particularly large stone objects, such as the two Ptolemaic limestone sarcophagi belonging to Pa-di-Inpw and Pa-di-Djehuti (figures 36, 120), were heavy and difficult to maneuver, and they showed the ability of these men to marshal skilled labor and unwieldy materials. Elite tomb chapels also made socio-political statements: officials had their numerous titles and family connections as well as their most illustrious achievements inscribed on

122

the walls of these chapels, linking themselves to wealthy state institutions and to higher members of society, particularly the royal family. Materials, too, held social significance: a New Kingdom head (figure 121), perhaps once belonging to a funerary statue of a nobleman, is made of granodiorite—a stone available exclusively through the royal quarrying monopoly. This object may have been a gift from the king himself, and it was probably displayed for the social and economic benefit of family members.

Many elites displayed their funerary wealth ostentatiously, making an obvious statement to those watching the funerary rituals in which masks

122. *Head and Chest from a Sarcophagus.* From Egypt. Roman Period, 4th century C.E. Terracotta, painted, 17 ½ x 17 ½ x 4 ½ in. (44.5 x 44.5 x 11.4 cm). Charles Edwin Wilbour Fund, 83.29

Terracotta sarcophagi could be hand modeled and quite individual, not following any established portrait style.

123. *Mummy Cartonnage of a Woman.* From Hawara, Egypt. Roman Period, 1st century C.E. Linen, gilded gesso, glass, faience, 22 $^{11}/_{16}$ x 14 $^{5}/_{8}$ x 7 $^{1}/_{2}$ in. (57.6 x 37.2 x 19 cm). Charles Edwin Wilbour Fund, 69.35

Some Roman Period mummy masks drew largely on classical style.

and coffins took the primary role. For example, the cartonnage mummy cover of a Roman woman of the first century C.E. (figure 123) visibly showcases her elite status through opulent gilding and glass inlay. The mummy mask of a man from the same century (figure 106) indicates that other individuals could not afford so much gilding. Other elites of the same period chose not to be as ostentatious in their funerary styles, selecting a more naturalistic painted death portrait, although they still made sure to include as much gold as they could, as on the encaustic painting of the man Demetrios of the Roman Period (figure 16).

As these various objects suggest, Egyptian funerary art is a key illustration of social inequality and limited choice within a complex society. The mere fact that most of the body containers in this book are painted, varnished, and even gilded clearly indicates that the high elite are tremendously over-represented in our modern museum collections. To put it simply: the vast majority of ancient Egyptians had *no* coffin or other funerary objects to speak of. Their own corpse was meant to provide them with a material existence after death and a vessel for their soul. Whether an individual could afford a richly made coffin, a modest body container, or only a simply prepared corpse, each of these different vessels provided the deceased with a material understanding of, and expectations for, the quality of his or her own afterlife. Many individuals unable to afford the real thing therefore included miniature or imitation versions of elite funerary materials, hoping for the same carryover of wealth in the afterlife, as seen in the New Kingdom pottery vessel painted to resemble expensive red granite (figure 92), presumably granting the dead owners more wealth in death than they had in life;[29] such objects were not only necessary to maintain one's socio-economic status in the afterlife, but might also have served to elevate it. Other Egyptians, however, made do with cheap pottery coffins, some of substandard craftsmanship (figure 122), because they could not afford wood, a commodity of some expense in ancient Egypt.

Usurpation and Reuse of Burial Goods

The demand for funerary arts had some ongoing consequences throughout the millennia. Most notably, the usurpation and reuse of burial goods was inevitable, given how important coffins, mummy masks, and canopic jars were to owners and family members—not only for the proper survival of the corpse, but also as a display of status within the funerary ritual. Coffins and other funerary arts were not freely available to all who wanted them.

124. *Coffin of the Lady of the House, Weretwahset, Reinscribed for Bensuipet.* From Deir el-Medina, Egypt. New Kingdom, early Dynasty 19, circa 1292–1190 B.C.E. Wood, painted, 24 13/16 x 12 13/16 x 76 3/16 in. (63 x 32.5 x 193.5 cm). Charles Edwin Wilbour Fund, 37.47Ea–b

This coffin combines the mummy board in "everyday dress" with the lid of the inner coffin, usually a separate piece, thus saving considerable effort and resources. More expensive sets included a separate mummy board that rested on top of the mummy and inside the coffin.

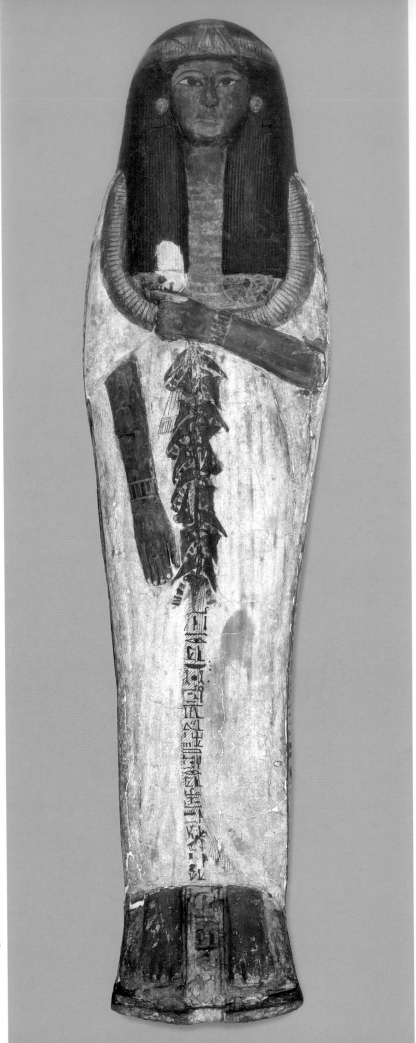

125

126

125. Side view of *Coffin of the Lady of the House, Weretwahset, Reinscribed for Bensuipet*

126. Detail of *Coffin of the Lady of the House, Weretwahset, Reinscribed for Bensuipet*

The name Bensuipet is written in black hieroglyphs contrasting with the green, blue, and red hieroglyphs visible underneath the black ones that spell Weretwahset's name. Adding the name of the second user of a reused coffin was essential for preserving the deceased in the netherworld. The details of how a coffin came to be reused are unclear, but reuse could have been the result of tomb robbery.

Even during times of prosperity, most Egyptians had no chance of saving up the necessary amount, and in times of economic scarcity, the competition to acquire a coffin was fierce, driving many to usurp and reuse the coffins of the buried dead.[30]

The usurpation of a coffin blurred the distinction between economic and religious functions by taking the religiously charged object out of the sphere of the sacred burial chamber and placing it back in the sphere of the commodity. Tomb robbery was an ancient profession in ancient Egypt, mentioned in instructional texts and pessimistic literature long before the New Kingdom.[31]

Coffin reuse was quite common during the Third Intermediate Period,[32] but the usurpation of funerary goods was already happening at the end of the New Kingdom, to which the Theban coffin of Weretwahset attests (figure 124). This Nineteenth Dynasty coffin was repainted for another woman, named Bensuipet, at either the end of the Twentieth Dynasty or the beginning of the Twenty-first. It is unknown how this kind of coffin reuse actually took place: were old coffins *sold* by Egyptian family members after exhuming them from common burial spaces generations after the death of the owner? Or were objects simply stolen, after socially supported tomb protection systems broke down, and then turned into commodities again? Usurpation was adaptive and innovative, probably relying on a variety of techniques to return a buried coffin to the commodity state.[33] In the Third Intermediate Period, even kings usurped and reused the funerary objects of much wealthier kings who had died before them,[34] indicating that usurpation involved a negotiation between theft and positive reassociation—essentially, an innovative conciliation between the principles of *ma'at*, or justice, and the need to incorporate religious powers into funerary objects.

Usurpation also reveals that Egyptian society as a whole placed more emphasis on the use of funerary materials in ritual and display contexts than it did on the permanent burial of those funerary objects with the dead.[35] Funerary objects were manipulated within ritual contexts to change the deceased into a form that could traverse the passage into the afterlife. Burial goods also provided the soul of the deceased with a material vessel— an earthly shape that could be pulled into the worldly sphere by living family members—so that they could offer to, and communicate with, the dead. For example, some statues found in the village of Deir el-Medina represent deceased family members; these ancestor busts were not placed in tombs, but rather in homes, in order to provide a material means of bringing the soul of the dead into the world of the living (see figures 127, 128). If material objects were thought necessary, even to some degree, to make transformation of the dead, and communication with the dead, possible, then usurpation became inevitable when the necessary objects could not be obtained in any other way.

The Social and Economic Meaning of Funerary Art

To use a very loose analogy, the Egyptian funeral can be compared to a modern wedding. A wedding is, among other things, a public display in

127

127. *Female Ancestral Bust.* From Deir el-Medina, Egypt. New Kingdom, Dynasty 18 to Dynasty 19, circa 1539–1190 B.C.E. Pottery, painted, 6 ⁵⁄₁₆ x 3 x 2 ⁵⁄₁₆ in. (16 x 7.6 x 5.8 cm). Charles Edwin Wilbour Fund, 61.49

Pottery ancestral busts were cheaper and easier to manufacture than limestone examples such as figure 128.

which the wealth and social position of a family can be shown to relatives, friends, and acquaintances by material means.[36] A wedding functions on many different levels. The ritual binds the couple together in the eyes of the community. But at the same time, the communal nature of the ritual also allows social and political networking to take place through shared meals and gift giving. And, of course, lavish displays of clothing, food, and drink traditionally associated with the wedding ritual communicate the economic capability and status of the bride's and groom's families.

In the same way, the Egyptian funeral functioned on many different levels: social, economic, and religious. Egyptology usually focuses on the religious aspects of death, in particular the traditional funerary beliefs and practices of the elites. However, by examining the real-world functionality of the funerary objects themselves, as in this essay, we can expose additional layers of meaning.

The underlying reality is that every funerary object in this exhibition was once commissioned, produced, and sold for a price before it became a part of any burial ceremony. Some of these funerary arts were even taken out of the burial context, recommoditized, and reused for other individuals because the demand for the object could not be met by any other means. Most funerary objects were at the center of public ritual displays, granting prestige and status to surviving family members as well as to the deceased in the next life. The socio-economic functions of funerary objects and their more familiar religious purposes were by no means mutually exclusive. It remains true, however, that social and economic factors dictated the quality, size, materials, and style of every funerary object produced in ancient Egypt, among them the prized artworks featured in this exhibition.

128. *Ancestral Bust of a Woman.* From Egypt. New Kingdom, late Dynasty 18 to early Dynasty 19, circa 1336–1279 B.C.E. Limestone, painted, 10 ¼ x 6 ⅛ x 3 ¾ in. (26 x 15.6 x 9.5 cm). Charles Edwin Wilbour Fund, 54.1

Busts of ancestors were kept in many homes as a memorial but also possibly to aid direct intervention by the spirit of the dead in the land of the living.

Notes to "How Much Did a Coffin Cost?"

1. For this translation of the Instruction of Hardjedef, see Miriam Lichtheim, *Ancient Egyptian Literature: A Book of Readings,* vol. 1: *The Old and Middle Kingdoms* (Berkeley, Los Angeles, and London: University of California Press, 1975), p. 58.

2. R. O. Faulkner and O. Goelet, *The Egyptian Book of the Dead: The Book of Going Forth by Day; The First Authentic Presentation of the Complete Papyrus of Ani* (San Francisco: James Wasserman, 1994), pl. 6.

3. Ibid., pl. 17.

4. M. L. Bierbrier, *The Tomb Builders of the Pharaohs* (London: British Museum Publications, 1982); Jaroslav Černý, *Community of Workmen at Thebes in the Ramesside Period* (Cairo: Institut Français d'Archéologie Orientale, 1973); Dominique Valbelle, *Les Ouvriers de la tombe: Deir el-Médineh à l'époque Ramesside* (Cairo: Institut Français d'Archéologie Orientale, 1985).

5. A. G. McDowell, *Village Life in Ancient Egypt: Laundry Lists and Love Songs* (Oxford: Oxford University Press, 1999).

6. Kathlyn M. Cooney, *The Cost of Death: The Social and Economic Value of Ancient Egyptian Funerary Art in the Ramesside Period* (Leiden: Egypto-logische Uitgaven, 2007).

7. Jac. J. Janssen, *Commodity Prices from the Ramessid Period: An Economic Study of the Village of Necropolis Workmen at Thebes* (Leiden: Brill, 1975).

8. S. Allam, *Hieratische Ostraka und Papyri aus der Ramessidenzeit,* 2 vols. (Tübingen: Im Selbstverlag des Herausgebers, 1973), vol. 1, pp. 101–02; Jaroslav Černý, *Catalogue des ostraca hiératiques non littéraires de Deir el Médineh,* 6 vols. (Cairo: Institut Français d'Archéologie Orientale, 1937–70), vol. 2, p. 9, pl. 18; Kenneth A. Kitchen, *Ramesside Inscriptions: Historical and Biographical,* 8 vols. (Oxford: Blackwell Publishers, 1969–90), vol. 6, p. 664; McDowell, *Village Life in Ancient Egypt,* p. 80.

9. Deir el-Medina craftsmen were paid 5.5 *khar* sacks of grain a month, more or less, which is equivalent to 11 *deben.* Jaroslav Černý, "Prices and Wages in Egypt in the Ramesside Period," *Cahiers d'histoire mondiale,* vol. 1 (1954), pp. 903–21; Janssen, *Commodity Prices*; Jac. J. Janssen, "Rations with Riddles II," *Göttinger Miszellen,* vol. 128 (1992), pp. 831–94.

10. Unpublished, after Černý Notebooks 45.85 and 107.16, with permission of the Griffith Institute, Oxford.

11. Allam, *Hieratische Ostraka und Papyri aus der Ramessidenzeit,* pp. 182–83; Jaroslav Černý and Alan H. Gardiner, *Hieratic Ostraca* (Oxford: Griffith Institute, 1957), p. 17, pl. 58, #3; Kitchen, *Ramesside Inscriptions,* vol. 6, pp. 255–56.

12. Jaroslav Černý and Georges Posener, *Papyrus hiératiques de Deir el-Médineh, Nos. I–XVII, Documents de fouilles,* 8 vols. (Cairo: Institut Français d'Archéologie Orientale, 1978–86), vol. 1, pp. 21–22, pl. 25; Kitchen, *Ramesside Inscriptions,* vol. 6, p. 672; E. F. Wente, *Letters from Ancient Egypt* (Atlanta: Scholars Press, 1990), pp. 168–69.

13. Kathlyn M. Cooney, "An Informal Workshop: Textual Evidence for Private Funerary Art Production in the Ramesside Period," in A. Dorn and T. Hofmann, eds., *Living and Writing in Deir el-Medine: Socio-Historical Embodiment of Deir el-Medine Texts* [University of Basel, July 2004]; *Aegyptiaca Helvetica* 19 (Basel: Schwabe Verlag, 2006).

14. Allam, *Hieratische Ostraka und Papyri aus der Ramessidenzeit,* pp. 72–73; Černý and Gardiner, *Hieratic Ostraca,* p. 16, pl. 54, #4; Wolfgang Helck, *Materialien zur Wirtschaftsgeschichte des Neuen Reiches,* 6 vols. (Wiesbaden: Verlag Otto Harrassowitz, 1961–69), vol. 5, p. 938; Kitchen, *Ramesside Inscriptions,* vol. 3, pp. 533–34; Kenneth A. Kitchen, *Ramesside Inscriptions: Translated and Annotated,* 3 vols. to date (Oxford: Blackwell Publishers, 1994–2003), vol. 3, p. 373; McDowell, *Village Life in Ancient Egypt,* p. 75; Jaana Toivari-Viitala, *Women at Deir el-Medina: A Study of the Status and Roles of the Female Inhabitants in the Workmen's Community during the Ramesside Period* (Leiden: Netherlands Institute for the Near East, 2001), p. 116; Wente, *Letters from Ancient Egypt,* p. 153.

15. Allam, *Hieratische Ostraka und Papyri aus der Ramessidenzeit,* pp. 105–06; Černý, *Catalogue des ostraca hiératiques non littéraires de Deir el Médineh,* vol. 3, p. 9, pl. 16; Helck, *Materialien zur Wirtschaftsgeschichte des Neuen Reiches,* vol. 3, p. 342;

Kitchen, *Ramesside Inscriptions*, vol. 6, pp. 157–58; Toivari-Viitala, *Women at Deir el-Medina*, p. 129.

16. Jac. J. Janssen and P. W. Pestman, "Burial and Inheritance in the Community of Necropolis Workmen at Thebes (Pap. Boulaq X and O. Petrie 16)," *Journal of the Economic and Social History of the Orient*, vol. 11 (1968), pp. 137–70.

17. Unpublished, after Černý, with kind permission of the Griffith Institute, Oxford.

18. Cooney, *The Cost of Death*.

19. Allam, *Hieratische Ostraka und Papyri aus der Ramessidenzeit*, pp. 201–02; Černý and Gardiner, *Hieratic Ostraca*, p. 18, pl. 62, #3; Kitchen, *Ramesside Inscriptions*, vol. 4, pp. 162–63.

20. Černý, *Catalogue des ostraca hiératiques non littéraires de Deir el Médineh*, vol. 5, p. 13, pl. 21; Kitchen, *Ramesside Inscriptions*, vol. 5, pp. 593–94; Toivari-Viitala, *Women at Deir el-Medina*, p. 128.

21. Unpublished, after Černý, with kind permission of the Griffith Institute, Oxford.

22. Kitchen, *Ramesside Inscriptions*, vol. 7, pp. 182–83.

23. Janssen, *Commodity Prices from the Ramessid Period*, p. 102, n. 6.

24. Nicholas Reeves, *The Complete Tutankhamun: The King, the Tomb, the Royal Treasure* (London: Thames & Hudson, 1990).

25. Herodotus, *The Histories*, trans. John Marincola (London: Penguin, 1972), vol. 2, pp. 85–89.

26. Kitchen, *Ramesside Inscriptions*, vol. 7, p. 322; Jesus Lopez, *Ostraca ieratici, Catalogo del Museo egizio di Torino* (Milan: Cisalpino-La Goliardica, 1978–84), vol. 3, p. 23, pl. 114.

27. From the buyer of the coffin.

28. Jaroslav Černý, *Ostraca hiératiques, Nos. 25501–25832: Catalogue général des antiquités égyptiennes du Musée du Caire* (Cairo: Institut Français d'Archéologie Orientale, 1935), pp. 35, 58, pl. 50.

29. John Baines and Peter Lacovara, "Burial and the Dead in Ancient Egyptian Society," *Journal of Social Archaeology*, vol. 2, no. 1 (2002), pp. 5–36.

30. Barry Kemp, *Ancient Egypt: Anatomy of a Civilization* (New York and London: Routledge, 1989), pp. 240–44; John H. Taylor, *Death and the Afterlife in Ancient Egypt* (Chicago: University of Chicago Press, 2001), pp. 178–82.

31. Evidence for tomb robbery goes back to the Predynastic Period. See Baines and Lacovara, "Burial and the Dead in Ancient Egyptian Society."

32. Andrzej Niwinski, *Twenty-first Dynasty Coffins from Thebes: Chronological and Typological Studies* (Mainz am Rhein: P. von Zabern, 1988), p. 57; Taylor, *Death and the Afterlife in Ancient Egypt*, p. 181. About 450 coffins dating to the Twenty-first or very early Twenty-second Dynasty have been identified by Niwinski, a time period only about 125 years in length. When this is compared to the number of known Ramesside coffins, which is just over 60, usurpation is the likely culprit.

33. Arjun Appadurai, "Introduction: Commodities and the Politics of Value," in Arjun Appadurai, ed., *The Social Life of Things: Commodities in Cultural Perspective* (Cambridge: Cambridge University Press, 1988).

34. See in particular the reuse of Ramesside royal coffins and sarcophagi by the Third Intermediate royal family at Tanis; J. P. M. Montet, *La Nécropole royale de Tanis*, 3 vols. (Paris: Commission des Fouilles de la Direction Général des Relations Culturelles, 1947–60).

35. Cooney, *The Cost of Death*. For this same idea, see Baines and Lacovara, "Burial and the Dead in Ancient Egyptian Society," p. 15: "From an early period, symbolic approaches and interpretations could bridge the gap between aspiration and reality. It is as if the outward appearance of mortuary ritual and provision could be more important than the provision itself."

36. See Vicki Howard, *Brides, Inc.: American Weddings and the Business of Tradition* (Philadelphia: University of Pennsylvania Press, 2006).

Further Reading

Allam, S. *Hieratische Ostraka und Papyri aus der Ramessidenzeit*, 2 vols. Tübingen: Im Selbstverlag des Herausgebers, 1973.

Altenmüller, Hartwig. "Bestattungs-ritual." In *Lexikon der Ägyptologie*, vol. 1. Edited by Wolfgang Helck and Eberhard Otto. Wiesbaden: Verlag Otto Harrassowitz, 1975.

Appadurai, Arjun. "Introduction: Commodities and the Politics of Value." In Arjun Appadurai, ed., *The Social Life of Things: Commodities in Cultural Perspective*. Cambridge: Cambridge University Press, 1986.

Assmann, Jan. *Death and Salvation in Ancient Egypt*. Translated from the German by David Lorton. Ithaca and London: Cornell University Press, 2005.

Baines, John, and Peter Lacovara. "Burial and the Dead in Ancient Egyptian Society." *Journal of Social Archaeology*, vol. 2, no. 1 (2002), pp. 5–36.

Bierbrier, M. L. *The Tomb Builders of the Pharaohs*. London: British Museum Publications, 1982.

Brier, Bob. *Egyptian Mummies: Unraveling the Secrets of an Ancient Art*. New York: William Morrow & Co., 1994.

Černý, Jaroslav. *Ostraca hiératiques, Nos. 25501–25832: Catalogue général des antiquités égyptiennes du Musée du Caire*. Cairo: Institut Français d'Archéologie Orientale, 1935.

———. *Catalogue des ostraca hiératiques non littéraires de Deir el Médineh*. 6 vols. Cairo: Institut Français d'Archéologie Orientale, 1937–70.

———. "Prices and Wages in Egypt in the Ramesside Period." *Cahiers d'histoire mondiale*, vol. 1 (1954), pp. 903–21.

———. *Community of Workmen at Thebes in the Ramesside Period*. Cairo: Institut Français d'Archéologie Orientale,1973.

———, and Alan H. Gardiner. *Hieratic Ostraca*. Oxford: Griffith Institute, 1957.

———, and Georges Posener. *Papyrus hiératiques de Deir el-Médineh, Nos. I–XVII, Documents de fouilles*. 8 vols. Cairo: Institut Français d'Archéologie Orientale, 1978–86.

Cooney, Kathlyn M. *The Cost of Death: The Social and Economic Value of Ancient Egyptian Funerary Art in the Ramesside Period*. Leiden: Brill, 2007.

David, Rosalie, and Rick Archbold. *Conversations with Mummies: New Light on the Lives of Ancient Egyptians*. London: HarperCollins, Madison Press, 2000.

Faulkner, R. O. *The Ancient Egyptian Pyramid Texts*. Oxford: Clarendon Press, 1969.

———. *The Ancient Egyptian Book of the Dead*. Edited by Carol Andrews. London: British Museum Publications, 1985.

———. *The Ancient Egyptian Coffin Texts*. Warminster: Aris & Phillips, 2004.

———, and O. Goelet. *The Egyptian Book of the Dead: The Book of Going Forth by Day; The First Authentic Presentation of the Complete Papyrus of Ani*. San Francisco: James Wasserman, 1994.

Grajetzki, Wolfram. *Burial Customs in Ancient Egypt: Life in Death for Rich and Poor*. London: Gerald Duckworth & Co., 2003.

Helck, Wolfgang. *Materialien zur Wirtschaftsgeschichte des Neuen Reiches*. 6 vols. Wiesbaden: Verlag Otto Harrassowitz, 1961–69.

Herodotus. *The Histories*. Translated by John Marincola. London: Penguin Books, 1972.

Hornung, Erik. *The Ancient Egyptian Books of the Afterlife*. Translated from the German by David Lorton. Ithaca and London: Cornell University Press, 1999.

Janssen, Jac. J. *Commodity Prices from the Ramessid Period: An Economic Study of the Village of Necropolis Workmen at Thebes*. Leiden: Brill, 1975.

———. "Rations with Riddles II," *Göttinger Miszellen*, vol. 128 (1992), pp. 831–94.

———, and P. W. Pestman. "Burial and Inheritance in the Community of Necropolis Workmen at Thebes (Pap. Boulaq X and O. Petrie 16)." *Journal of the Economic and Social History of the Orient*, vol. 11 (1968), pp. 137–70.

Kemp, Barry. *Ancient Egypt: Anatomy of a Civilization*. London and New York: Routledge, 1989.

Kitchen, Kenneth A. *Ramesside*

Inscriptions: Historical and Biographical. 8 vols. Oxford: Blackwell Publishers, 1969–90.

———. *Ramesside Inscriptions: Translated and Annotated.* 3 vols. to date. Oxford: Blackwell Publishers, 1994–2003.

Lichtheim, Miriam. *Ancient Egyptian Literature: A Book of Readings.* 3 vols. Berkeley, Los Angeles, and London: University of California Press, 1973–78.

Lopez, Jesus. *Ostraca ieratici, Catalogo del Museo egizio di Torino*, vol. 3, fasc. 1-4. Milan: Cisalpino-La Goliardica, 1978–84.

McDowell, A. G. *Village Life in Ancient Egypt: Laundry Lists and Love Songs.* Oxford: Oxford University Press, 1999.

Montet, J. P. M. *La Nécropole royale de Tanis.* 3 vols. Paris: Commission des Fouilles de la Direction Général des Relations Culturelles, 1947–60.

Niwinski, Andrzej. *Twenty-first Dynasty Coffins from Thebes: Chronological and Typological Studies.* Mainz am Rhein: P. von Zabern, 1988.

Reeves, Nicholas. *The Complete Tutankhamun: The King, the Tomb, the Royal Treasure.* London: Thames & Hudson, 1990.

Taylor, John H. *Death and the Afterlife in Ancient Egypt.* Chicago: University of Chicago Press, 2001.

Toivari-Viitala, Jaana. *Women at Deir el-Medina: A Study of the Status and Roles of the Female Inhabitants in the Workmen's Community during the Ramesside Period.* Leiden: Netherlands Institute for the Near East, 2001.

Valbelle, Dominque. *Les Ouvriers de la tombe: Deir el-Médineh à l'époque Ramesside.* Cairo: Institut Français d'Archéologie Orientale, 1985.

Wente, E. F. *Letters from Ancient Egypt.* Atlanta: Scholars Press, 1990.

Brooklyn Museum
Board of Trustees 2007–8

Index

Page numbers in *italics* indicate illustrations.